COUNTRY HARDBALL

THE AUTOBIOGRAPHY OF ENOS "COUNTRY" SLAUGHTER

Enos Slaughter
with
Kevin Reid

COUNTRY
HARDBALL

The Autobiography of
Enos "Country" Slaughter

Enos Slaughter
with
Kevin Reid

Tudor Publishers, Inc.   Greensboro

Country Hardball

The Autobiography of Enos "Country" Slaughter

Copyright © 1991 by Enos B. Slaughter and Kevin Reid.

Library of Congress Cataloging-in-Publication Data

Slaughter, Enos, 1916-
    Country hardball : the autobiography of Enos "Country" Slaughter /
Enos Slaughter with Kevin Reid. -- 1st ed.
        p.   cm.
    ISBN 0-936389-23-0 : $18.95
    1. Slaughter, Enos, 1916-   . 2. Baseball players--United States-
-Biography.   I. Reid, Kevin, 1947-   . II. Title.
GV865.S53A3   1991
796.357'092--dc20
[B]
                                                                91-1790?
                                                                     CIP

First Edition
Printed in the United States of America
Frontispiece: Sporting News

ISBN 0-936389-23-0
1 2 3 4 5 6 7 8 9

Dedication

For my daughters: Patricia, Gaye, Sharon and Rhonda.

—E.S.

To the memory of my parents, Ruby K. and George A. Reid.

—K.B.R.

1

I am not ashamed to admit that I go all the way back to the covered-wagon days. April 27, 1916, may not have been part of the covered-wagon era in cities like New York or St. Louis, but there sure weren't many automobiles around Allensville Township, near present-day Roxboro, in the northern central area of North Carolina, where I was born that day on the 90-acre farm of Lonie and Zadok Slaughter. That was when doctors made house calls. My middle name was after Dr. Bradsher who delivered me. My first name, Enos, was actually derived from a word in the Bible that means man.

Both of my parents came from farm families in the area. My mother's family, the Gentrys, traced their ancestry to England. The Slaughters were of German descent. My mother's family has been in this country since two Gentry brothers came to Virginia as Redcoats to put a stop to Bacon's Rebellion. It was years later that the Slaughter family arrived in Pennsylvania and Americanized the family name. By the time my grandfather Absolom Gentry migrated to this area of Person County where I still live, there were plenty of Slaughters farming this North Carolina land.

The Slaughters and the Gentrys got to know each other right well. Ab, as his friends called him, operated the largest general store in the area east of Roxboro. The Slaughters not only depended upon him for their sugar, salt, pepper, molasses and kerosene, but they also admired him as a progressive farmer. You see, Grandfather Gentry was the first farmer in these parts to harvest his wheat with a McCormick reaper.

While the Gentrys were merchants and trendsetters, the Slaughters were athletes. Besides his farming, Pa played semi-pro baseball. He was a bare-handed catcher and a barefooted one, too.

I guess Ma figured that a guy who wasn't afraid to handle speeding baseballs without the protection of a catcher's mitt or even shoes, had what it took to handle droughts, floods and anything else that could get in the way of a farmer. They married and settled on a piece of Slaughter property that was to become my first home. Like most farm families, theirs was to be large. By the time I arrived, I had already been preceded by Daniel in 1909, Hayward in 1911, and Carlton in 1913. I was followed by my sister Helen in 1918 and Robert, the sixth and last, in 1923.

Not very long after following my older brothers in birth, I followed them to the fields, where, like them, I was put to work. Besides milking the four cows on the family farm, we also raised our own corn and wheat. This enabled us to produce cornbread from scratch. From the wheat, we also made flour to carry to the mills. We would cut the wheat with a cradle and then hand-tie it and stack it, before throwing it into the combine.

When farm prices weren't the best, we had to wear triplepatch overalls, but we sure never had to worry about going hungry. You can bet that we always had plenty to eat. For breakfast, we'd have fried potatoes and homemade biscuits, covered with a thick gravy. Since the family raised hogs, there was also country fresh sausage and good old smoked country ham. Our diet also consisted heavily of buttermilk, turnip salad, and fatback.

The farm was not the sole source of our food supply. My mother and dad were both avid fishermen, and they passed the fondness for this activity on to their children. Fishing has been a part of my life for as long as I can recall, and my early memories of it are among the happiest that I have. We always looked forward to the excursions we would take along with two or three other families, sometimes 18 to 20 people in all, for an outing of fishing and camping. We would load into our covered wagons and head out eight to ten miles or so to a creek, where we would catch different kinds of fish, including bass, carp, bream, catfish, pike, and one we called roundfish. We would then take the fish, along with any frogs and snapping turtles we caught, and clean them right there on the river bank and cook them over a campfire. We then ate our catch along with cornbread and other homemade delights.

In addition to farming and fishing, we also got our food by hunting. As a small child, I joined my father and brothers to hunt rabbits, a favorite item on our family menu. No, I didn't shoot them. At the time, there wasn't enough money to buy me a gun. It was my job to throw rocks at them. Needless to say, in order to do that, I had to throw straight and hard. This built my arm up so that later, as a rightfielder, I could throw baseballs hard and accurately enough to nail baserunners at home plate.

I also have great memories of the hunting expeditions in the nearby forests which I took along with my father and brothers. One of them, which I will discuss later, led to one of my darkest memories. Despite that, to this day, I still enjoy recalling the thrill I experienced as a youngster when I bagged my first wild turkey. We were actually in the woods listening for squirrels at the time, when damned if a 22-pound gobbler didn't run right by me and my single-barrelled shotgun. That incident turned out to be a lesson to me that you never know when to expect opportunity.

My family made the most of every opportunity to hunt. In order to get more variety into our diet, we even hunted on our fishing trips. Near creeks and streams, we would gig for frogs and trap snapping turtles. Those turtles really have a mean bite if you let one get hold of you, but, I'll tell you, they're sure good eating.

Those were really good times. I think people enjoyed life more back then than they do today. Neighbors didn't mind pitching in and helping people get things done. This spirit of togetherness did really abound in the fall, when the corn was ready to be harvested. About fifteen of us would get together and have ourselves a cornshucking. Once the husks were removed from the stalks, we put them in cribs in the barn, so that the mules, cows, and pigs had food for the winter.

And in the spring, 15 or 20 neighbors went into the forests for a communal wood-chopping. The most practical time to cut firewood might be in the fall, but most wood was burned in curing tobacco. Needless to say, that was before the days of oil burners or gas burners. Also, in the spring the sap was down, making the wood easier to burn. One day we all would pitch in together and chop wood for one family, and the next day, we'd all team up and do it for another. Then, the following day those families would chop wood for us.

The next day, we would all meet back at that farm and cut the logs into shorter sections. That's when we'd have wood-chopping contests. It's a wonder none of us ever lost a foot or anything the way we were chopping away at such a furious pace to win those contests. I can't help but think that swinging those axes helped me in my instincts as a batter in professional baseball. There's no doubt that working in the barns kept me in shape.

Even though I threw and did just about everything else right-handed, I felt more comfortable chopping wood lefthanded. The only other thing I did lefthanded was swing a baseball bat.

While the men were chopping wood, the women would be in the farm house. They'd be cooking all morning. At noon, they would ring that old dinner bell. We'd head for the house to enjoy our feast. Even the mules would stop whatever they were doing at the sound of that bell and bray with delight. They knew it was time for them to eat, too.

Working on a farm and participating in corn shuckings and wood-choppings not only helped me and my brothers improve our physical and athletic capabilities, it also taught us the value of teamwork. My parents, both sports enthusiasts all of their lives, encouraged not only their sons, but also their daughter to partici-pate in different athletic activities. Despite all the time and energy needed to operate the farm, sports played a major role in the lives of the Slaughters. While crop and livestock production was nec-essary for our family's survival, all work ceased when one of us was scheduled to play in an organized baseball, football, or bas-ketball game. In a local sports contest, if Helen, one of my broth-ers, or I was playing, the rest of the Slaughters came to watch.

My father taught us how to play ball. He stood five feet seven inches tall and weighed just 145 pounds, but his hustle and deter-mination more than made up for his lack of size. Those bare hands that had caught smoking fastballs were still strong enough to chop down ash trees and carve bats out of the wood for his kids.

My first memories of going to ballgames were with the family by horse and buggy. Our first automobile was a 1927 Ford Model-T. But when the Depression hit, we couldn't afford gasoline for the Model-T, so we rode in what we called "Hoovercarts." These were actually engineless automobile chassis hooked to a mule. On special occasions, we all piled into whatever vehicle we were using at the time and rode 25 miles south to Durham to watch professional baseball. At those Bulls games in the old Piedmont League, I began to realize that it was my life's ambition to become a professional baseball player.

As soon as Daniel was old enough to become an outfielder and pitcher for the Longhurst industrial league team, the whole family would go to all of his games. Then Hayward joined the Ca-Vel team at the Collins and Aikman textile mill. On that team, he would soon be followed by Carlton, then me, and finally, Robert.

The Model-T was also used to take the Slaughters to watch one of their own play high school football and basketball. I was a starting forward on the basketball team at Allensville High School. One game I scored 28 points, which is not too bad for a guy who was only five-foot-nine.

Just before my senior year, I transferred to Bethel Hill High School so I could play football, even though it meant that I had to walk two miles to catch a bus and then ride ten miles, when Allensville High School was only a mile and a half away. I knew it was all worthwhile when I met Hulo Powell, who became my high school sweetheart.

On the football team, I was the fullback, did the kicking and also ran back punt returns. One Friday night, at Graham, I broke through the defensive line only to have one of their linemen fall on my head and knock me out. At least that's what they told me. I never remembered it. For that matter, I never remembered anything at all until the following Sunday afternoon. By then, I had been delirious for two days.

Despite my football and basketball exploits, baseball was still my best sport. As a second baseman, I was already considered to be a better player than my older brothers, who by this time were playing semi-pro ball for mill teams in the area. I hit .575 my senior year in high school.

I didn't follow any particular baseball team in those days. In fact, I didn't keep up with major league baseball at all when I was young. We didn't get a newspaper back in those days. I just loved baseball, period. I loved to play the game.

My accomplishments in baseball and football led to an athletic scholarship offer from Guilford College in Greensboro. This pleased my dad, who wanted me to continue my education. But I didn't share those feelings. My mind was set on going to work for the mill and continuing to play second base for the company team. After he and I went back and forth a few times over the matter, he finally relented, saying: "All right. If you can do what you want often enough, you ought to be happy."

This really did make me happy because it was the best chance I had to realize my ambition of becoming a professional ballplayer. I wasn't even thinking about the major leagues. I would have been happy playing for a team like the Durham Bulls, just as long as I could make a living playing the game.

After that season, our manager, B. B. Mangum, took the team up to Washington to see the Senators play the New York Yankees. Babe Ruth was playing that day and, yes, he hit one out. It was home run number 708 for the Bambino. it also turned out to be the last one that he ever hit for the Yankees.

As Babe Ruth's career as a professional ballplayer was ending, it was time for Enos Slaughter's to begin. Ruth's last year as a player was my first in the minor leagues. It all started shortly after I came back from Washington on that trip with the Ca-Vel team.

My first 25 years in pro baseball were sandwiched between two men named Fred Haney. The first Fred Haney that affected my life was the sports editor of *The Durham Morning Herald*. He had been following the Ca-Vel team that I played second base for.

And, he was a good friend of Oliver French, a relative of the already-famous Branch Rickey.

Rickey is credited with the idea of developing talent for a major league baseball club. Before he started this practice, major league teams didn't purchase minor leaguers until they were ready for the big time. He did this when he was managing the St. Louis Cardinals. By the time I finished high school, Branch no longer managed the Cardinals, but he was the general manager of the team, and also oversaw the vast farm system he had created.

French owned the Cardinals farm team in Greensboro, and was all ears when his buddy Fred Haney told him about Morris Briggs, Lester James, and me from the Ca-Vel team. Thanks to that newspaperman, the three of us each got a letter from the Cardinals inviting us to attend a tryout at Greensboro's War Memorial Stadium in September of 1934. Forget about any bonus money. If we made the team and were signed to a contract, our expenses would be paid. If not, we were out transportation costs. That was good enough for me. It was what I had been gearing my life for.

The tryout camp lasted 10 days. The man in charge was Billy Southworth, who had spent about a dozen years as a major league outfielder and had managed the Cardinals in 1929, his last year as a player. Southworth saw some major league potential in me, but not as a second baseman. He said that I looked clumsy at the keystone position. Fortunately, I could throw the ball with enough power to have potential as an outfielder. I didn't exactly bowl them over with my skills out there at the beginning. Neither did Briggs, who was also trying to land an outfield spot. But we both seemed to show Southworth enough potential to be asked back for another look the next spring.

That winter brought another important first in my life, my marriage to my high school sweetheart, Hulo Powell. We lived on the twenty dollars per week I was earning splitting cloth on the night shift at Ca-Vel. Still, I think she was happier then than at any other time in our brief marriage. She was in love with Enos Slaughter the farm boy, not Enos Slaughter the professional baseball player, and the life in that sport would ultimately lead to the end of that marriage.

However, it was my professional baseball career that almost ended the following spring, training in Asheville. There, I had been judged to be too slow afoot, and the Cardinals were about to give me my release, when Southworth took me to the outfield and asked, "Did you know that you've been running flat-footed? Why don't you try running on your toes?"

For the next three days, I practiced running in the outfield, and was able to increase my speed to first base by four steps. Those three days saved a long baseball career.

I was assigned to the Martinsville Redbirds of the class D Bi-State League. That led to my first dealings with Branch Rickey, who had been a catcher for the St. Louis Browns and the New York Highlanders before I was born. Later, he managed in St. Louis, first for the Browns, and later for the Cardinals. After the 1925 season, Cardinals owner Sam Breadon, who had acquired his wealth through a Pierce-Arrow automobile dealership, made star second baseman Rogers Hornsby the manager and Rickey the general manager. It was as an executive that Branch was to really make his mark in the game of baseball. He signed me to a contract of $75 per month.

I moved to Martinsville, a town in southern Virginia. It was only about 60 miles from Roxboro, but it might as well have been a thousand. I didn't have a car then, so I moved to a rooming house about two blocks from the ballpark. My rent was five dollars a week. Not bad, but then again, I couldn't afford more on a salary of $75 a month. The landlords were nice, but living with Mr. and Mrs. Cook was not like living with my wife. And not only did I miss Hulo, but I also was away from my parents and brothers and sister for the first time.

I was really lonely that first year away from home. I sat awake in that rooming house unable to sleep from homesickness. Then, too, it felt strange not to be working in the spring fields for the first time in my life. In my new working environment, the baseball field, I had other changes to deal with. I had to get used to right field. I did like throwing out baserunners. It was like throwing rocks at rabbits when I was a kid too young for a gun. Still, I had defensive problems out there. I was all right on fly balls, but I sure had my problems with grounders.

I hit .275 that year, with over a third of my hits, including 18 homers, going for extra bases. I struck out a bit my first year as a professional because, at the time, I hadn't really learned how to use the strike zone to my advantage and was swinging at some bad balls. My outfield play was all right on fly balls, but grounders were a real weakness. I dreaded having a ground ball hit to me in game situations, and actually had coaches hit me practice balls on the ground rather than in the air to help work on this problem. Things got to the point where I would just get down on both knees and, if the ball were to miss my glove, hope that it would hit my legs or my chest.

I was the only player from that team to make the major leagues. My teammate from Ca-Vel, Morris Briggs, was a left-handed hitter and thrower who stood 6'2" tall and weighed 195 pounds. I have always felt that he would have made an ideal first baseman, but he was too homesick to stay in Martinsville. Away from my wife and all my friends and family from Roxboro, I got homesick too, but I had made up my mind that I was going to be a professional baseball player.

Still, following the season, I was glad to get back to Roxboro, back to Hulo and to my nightshift cloth-splitting job at the mill. In the daytime, I kept busy splitting wood. These wood-choppings kept me in shape.

Spring training in 1936 was held at Albany, Georgia, where the Cardinals had a camp for five minor league teams. That's when I first caught the attention of Eddie Dyer, a Texan who had originally made a name for himself as an all-around athlete at Rice University. The little southpaw was signed by St. Louis, but never amounted to much as a pitcher in the major leagues. He spent parts of six seasons with St. Louis, pitching in 69 games and winning 15 while losing 15. By 1927, Branch Rickey felt that he could no longer get big leaguers out, but thought the Texan could develop big league talent. By this time, Dyer was 35 years old. He in turn took an interest in me and asked if he could have me as the right fielder for the Columbus, Georgia team he was managing in the

South Atlantic League. Rickey was generous enough to raise my salary to $100 per month.

Even though it was also nicknamed the Sally League, this was not the one known as the South Atlantic League today. Today's Sally League, formerly the Western Carolinas League, has several cities in North and South Carolina, but back then all the teams were located in Georgia or Florida, with the exception of the Columbia, South Carolina club.

Once again, Hulo stayed behind in Roxboro, while I got a room in a boarding house located within walking distance of the clubhouse. My mood wasn't the best when I moved into that city in western Georgia.

Deep down inside I wondered if I was about to reach the end of my brief career as a pro ballplayer. After all, my older brothers were already finished as minor leaguers. Daniel was a good pitcher, and I think he could have probably made it to the big leagues, but he just couldn't make a go of it on a minor league salary, and went back to Roxboro.

Hayward had been a good first baseman, but Carlton had been the older brother that had the folks in Person County talking. He was an unusual catcher because he could run. When a batter hit a ground ball, Carlton would spring out of his backstop position and hustle to first base. Often, before the batter reached first on such a grounder, there would be Carlton, with all that catching gear on him, waiting behind the bag to back up the throw. He played for Sanford (North Carolina) one year in a Class D Tobacco State League, but that was the end of baseball for him.

So, in my second year in the Cardinals farm system, I wondered if I too might be joining my brothers back on the farm. I turned 20 in April, but played like a man ready to be retired to pasture during the first part of the season. My bad habits stuck, and the extra base hits weren't falling in. I'd swing at pitches so far out of the strike zone that pitchers didn't bother to throw me anything over the plate.

In right field, I was having a hard time handling ground balls. They seemed to take a different type of bounce than I was used to as a second baseman. As far as throwing went, I felt even then that

I had a good arm, but I didn't help the team by trying to throw out every baserunner instead of concentrating on getting the ball to the cut-off man.

My state of mind reached a low point one Savannah night in June. With the bases loaded, I struck out. Dyer had been patient with me, but this was more than he could take. It wasn't just that I struck out with the bases full. It was the way I struck out.

"You jumped a foot in the air trying to hit that last pitch," Dyer fumed. "That's why you're hitting .220."

Standing in right field in the bottom half of that inning, all I could think about was Dyer's anger, my latest strikeout and that pathetic .220 average. When the inning came to an end, I trotted back toward the dugout, then slowed down to a walk. When I reached the dugout steps, there to greet me again was Eddie Dyer, with an even angrier expression on his face.

"What's the matter, son? Are you too tired to run all the way?" he asked, in a voice coated with ice. "If so, then I'll get you some help."

That changed my life right there. From that moment on, Enos Slaughter never loafed on a baseball field. I can't say I was in any better a mood when it was time for me to go back to right field, but I hightailed it out there as fast as I could. From then on, I ran full speed to my position once my foot hit the top step of the dug-out, and I ran just as fast until I reached the dugout coming back. Those words Dyer said to me that night never left me.

After the game, I returned to the rooming house, but I couldn't go to sleep. I thought about what Dyer had said, and I thought about the things I had been doing wrong. I realized that nobody gave a damn about how sorry I felt for myself. I also figured that, the way I had been playing, I wasn't a help to my team. I wondered if I was going to be sent back down. I finally decided that I had to have a talk with my manager.

As I watched the sun rise through my window, I couldn't wait until it was time to go to the ballpark. I got there before Dyer arrived that day, and when he did, it was my turn to approach him.

"Skip," I said to the manager who was so exasperated with me the night before. "I know that you've got to get rid of me, but please don't send me back to Martinsville."

Eddie just smiled, motioned for me to sit down, and told me something that floored me. "Son," he said, "if you can overcome just two things, you have a good chance to go to the major leagues."

I couldn't believe what I was hearing. Here I was, preparing myself for the worst, and my manager was telling me that I had a chance to make it to the top. I had never even dreamed of being a big league ballplayer before.

"You've only got to learn that there's a strike zone at home plate and, in the infield, a cut-off man to handle relays," he continued. "Concentrate on getting a good ball at the plate and, in the outfield, stop trying to use your arm on nonstop throws."

This bit of encouragement and basic advice turned my mood from despair and frustration to optimism and enthusiasm. I had never before given thought to ever being a major league ballplayer. Starting at that point, however, I was determined to become a St. Louis Cardinal. I now had more desire, more determination, more willpower. I worked on the mechanics and kept the hustle going full speed ahead. This began to show on the field and in the box scores. Even though I was still wary of ground balls, my throws back to the infield were more accurate. My batting average rose over a hundred points during the second half of the season: I finished the year at .325.

Though my 1936 season at Columbus had gone from terrible to terrific, the following fall, while I was back in Roxboro, turned out to be just the opposite for Hulo and me. A daughter, Rebecca Ann, was born to us on October 23. But we lost her only six days later on October 29. It was a bleak and painful winter.

Perhaps more than anything else that helped me along during that mournful off-season was the newly discovered hope that I had for a major league career. I concentrated as much as possible that winter on how I was going to prove to the Cardinals organization that I belonged in the major leagues.

I must have made my sorrow add to my determination when I returned to spring training for the 1937 season. This time, I went to Daytona Beach to train with the big league club. It was my first chance to meet the members of the famed Gas House Gang that had won the 1934 World Series as well as the hearts of baseball fans from all over. The legendary Dizzy Dean was there, along with his brother Paul. And the 43-year-old Jesse "Pop" Haines and other future Hall-of-Farmers Joe Medwick and Johnny Mize. And, of course, the manager Frankie Frisch, who by then at the age of 38 was winding down his playing career as a second baseman.

Two other members of that squad's infield, shortstop Leo Durocher and third baseman Don Gutteridge, had managerial careers ahead of them, but I was mainly concerned with the outfield, where I was trying to win a spot. Joe Medwick, who the year before had hit 64 doubles to break the National League record and batted a cool .351 while also leading the League in hits, had a lock on the left field job. Terry Moore, who was to become my best friend in baseball, was set as the starting centerfielder (as he would be for years to come). The opening was a part-time one in right, where Rickey and Frisch were looking for a lefthanded hitter to platoon with Pepper Martin.

As it turned out, all Frisch wanted at the time was a look at me before sending me back down for more seasoning. Even though I had experienced the birth and death of a child, I had yet to reach my twenty-first birthday, and to the established major leaguers in camp, I was just a fresh kid who didn't know his way around. It seemed like every time I stepped up to the plate for batting practice, some of the older fellows would yell something like, "Go to the outfield, you fresh busher! We'll let you know when it's time for you to hit."

My time to hit didn't come very often in Daytona that spring. I think I came to bat only once, in an exhibition game. More attention was paid to Don Padgett, another rookie from North Carolina, who had a few years in age and minor league experience on me. When the Cardinals left Daytona to finish their spring training in Cuba, I was shipped to De Land, Florida, to train with the organization's American Association farm club, which was based in Columbus, Ohio. Meanwhile, Padgett went south with the big club and wound up spending that season platooning with Martin.

Despite my chance to spend time with the likes of Dizzy, Daffy, Ducky, Pop, the Fordham Flash, the Big Cat, the Lip, the Wild Hoss of the Osage and other folk heroes of the day, it was a relief for me to get back among mere mortals like Johnny Rizzo, Mort Cooper, Bill McGee, Dick Siebert, Nelson Potter and Skeeter Webb, whose days as major leaguers were ahead of them. Given a chance to play by my new manager Burt Shotton, I responded with a .418 average in the fifteen games or so in spring training as a Columbus Red Bird. Not all of that was against minor league pitching. I got three hits off Paul Dean to help us beat the Cardinals though, unfortunately, it turned out that at the tender age of 23, Daffy was already on his way out after straining his arm in spring training the year before. Still, my performance in that game was enough for Shotton to ask Rickey for permission to keep me on his American Association team, thus enabling me to skip Class A baseball. Eddie Dyer, having managed me the year before, told Shotton that he didn't think I was ready for double-A baseball, as the American Association was classified at the time. Shotton replied that anyone who had hit the way he had seen me hit, was going north with him if he had anything to say about it. At Shotton's request, Nick Cullop, who had been the team's rightfielder in 1936, was sold to Sacramento despite the fact that Cullop, who had bounced around the majors in the late twenties and early thirties, lived in Ohio and was very popular with the Columbus fans.

If Dyer had turned my baseball career around, Shotton kept it going in the right direction. He had been the St. Louis Browns starting centerfielder from 1911 through 1917, and later was a reserve outfielder for the crosstown Cards. Before returning to the Cardinals organization, he had managed the Philadelphia Phillies for six seasons and had coached for the Cincinnati Reds. More importantly, he took an immediate liking to this determined but naive kid from the Allensville Township. From the moment of our first meeting, he started calling me "Country Boy." That was fine with me because he also called on me to be his starting rightfielder.

We started the season off at Indianapolis, where I got nine hits in three games, and moved on to Louisville, where I managed nine more hits in the next three games. Then, we went home to Columbus for a week, and I couldn't buy myself a base hit. I was afraid that Shotton was going to decide that Dyer was right and send me down to Class A ball or, at least, bench me. To my pleasant surprise, he stuck with me as his everyday rightfielder as the team went back on the road.

Shotton's confidence in me, Dyer's advice to me, and my own determination to become a major leaguer all came together as the Red Birds travelled to Minneapolis, St. Paul, Kansas City, Milwaukee and Toledo. Waiting for the right pitch and making the most of my opportunity to play, I returned from that road trip leading the league in hitting.

Adding to my satisfaction was the fact that the team was in first place. Unlike my first two teams in the Cardinals farm system, this one was loaded with future major leaguers. Other hot hitters on the club were leftfielder Johnny Rizzo and Dick Siebert, who played first base. Both would have major league starting jobs in other organizations by the next season. Rounding out the outfield, which was considered to be the hardest-hitting, best-fielding and strongest-throwing in the American Association that year, was Lynn King, who had spent some time with the Cardinals the previous two seasons. Complementing Siebert in the infield were shortstop Jimmy "Skeeter" Webb, who the following year would begin an 11-year American League career; third baseman Justin Stein, who in 1938 would have a brief fling at the big time with the Philadelphia Phillies and Cincinnati Reds, and second baseman Jimmy Jordan, who during the previous four seasons had seen a lot of action as the Brooklyn Dodgers' utility infielder.

Others on that squad with major league experience included catcher Jack Crouch, a former St. Louis Brown and Cincinnati Red, and pitcher Ed Heusser who, like King, had been with the Cardinals the previous couple of years.

Although Heusser was to return to the majors and lead all National League pitchers in ERA while pitching for Cincinnati during the wartime season of 1944, he was not that effective on the Red Bird pitching staff of 1937. More successful for Shotton were future Cardinals Max Macon, Bill McGee, Max Lanier, Mort Cooper and John Chambers, as well as Nelson Potter, whose future on the mound was primarily in the American League.

While 1936 had been the year I first thought I had a shot at playing baseball in the majors, 1937 became the year in which I knew I would make it. I held on to my lead for the batting title as the Red Birds stayed in first place. I was named to the American Association All-Star team along with my Columbus teammates Rizzo, Siebert, Macon and McGee.

As I continued to reinforce the faith my manager had shown in me since spring training, I also gained popularity with the Columbus fans. My hustling to and from my position in right field, as well as the fact that I was leading the team in home runs and several other offensive departments, was making them forget their local favorite Nick Cullop, who was known affectionately to the fans as "Tomato Face." Recognizing my popularity, Robert Hooey, sports editor of the *Ohio State Journal,* decided to run a contest for his newspaper's readers to select a nickname for me. Hundreds of names were sent in, but I was the sole judge of the contest. I decided to stick with "Country," a shortened version of the nickname Shotton had hung on me during spring training. Despite another reporter in the area writing that I had hayseed sticking out of my ears, I was proud of the fact that I'd grown up on a farm. From that moment on, "Country" has always been my nickname to baseball fans and the press, but, other than Shotton, few of my associates have ever called me that. Later on, a few of the writers would call me "Bosco" or "Bake," but most of my teammates just called me Enos or shortened it a letter to Eno.

Besides being proud of my rural background, I was proud to be the first rookie to lead the American Association in batting. And, by season's end, 1 had racked up some pretty impressive numbers, with a .382 average, 245 hits, 26 home runs, 122 RBI'S, 147 runs and 18 stolen bases.

Our team continued its winning ways throughout the season. Our main competition came from the Toledo Mud Hens and the Minneapolis Millers, who were feeding the Boston Red Sox. We finished the season with a 90-64 record, a game ahead of the Mud Hens and three ahead of the Millers. The regular season championship was great for our egos, and it wasn't too bad for our pocketbooks either. The first act of George Trautman after he became president of the American Association that September was to sign a check for $4,000 and present it to our club to divide among its players.

2

In 1938, I went to spring training with the Cardinals for the second time, but that year, it was at the new Al Lang Field, in St. Petersburg instead of Daytona Beach. Today, over a half-century later, the Cardinals still conduct their spring training in St. Petersburg.

Dizzy, Ducky, and all of the rest of the characters were there from the previous spring training except for "The Lip." Frisch wanted Durocher out. He supposedly had told Mr. Rickey that it was either "him or me." I couldn't tell you why he did that. I was just a rookie then and I figured I was better off not asking questions.

I think that if Frank really did give Branch that ultimatum, it could very well have cost him his own hide. I think we could have won more games with Leo at shortstop and Don Gutteridge at third than we did with Gutteridge at short and Joe Stripp at third. Stripp was part of the deal the Cardinals made for Durocher. Dodgers general manager Larry MacPhail was more than happy to unload Jersey Joe to us. He had already replaced him at the Dodgers' hot corner with a guy from Oakland named Harry Arthur Lavagetto, better known as Cookie.

Dizzy, a Southern boy from rural Arkansas, seemed to take a liking to me. He liked my nickname, "Country," even though very few of the players called me that. And he seemed to like my work habits and probably appreciated the fact that, at the time, I wasn't opening my mouth too much.

Much more attention was being paid to the other "Jersey Joe." Medwick was better known as "Muscles" or "Ducky Wucky." It is not unheard of for a candy bar to be named after a baseball player, but have you ever heard of one that was named after a minor leaguer? That's exactly what had happened in the early '30s when Houston was the top St. Louis farm club. The "Ducky-Wucky" bar was made and sold in that city after fans compared his walk to that of the waddling bird.

Medwick hated the nickname. He preferred instead to be called the more complimentary "Muscles," but he didn't mind the royalties he was receiving from the candy. He liked to tell us younger players to be like him and go after those "base hits and buckarinos."

Our leftfielder was considered the best hitter in the National League at the time. He was coming off as good a year as anybody can have. Joe's imperialistic personality was also in full bloom. As a kid in Carteret, New Jersey, he had been an "All-Everything" in sports. After being the toast of New Jersey and turning down a football scholarship to Notre Dame, he had no trouble receiving continued adulation while coming up in the Cardinals farm system. Unfortunately for him, a bad back that spring may have ultimately cost him some buckarinos.

Meanwhile, The Big Cat showed up looking like a fat cat. Coming off a year when he had hit .364, Mize reported to spring training with a few extra pounds under his belt.

There was talk about sending me back to the American Association for more seasoning, but I had a great spring and I was attracting interest from the other major league teams, especially the Chicago Cubs, who had reportedly offered the Cardinals $100,000 for me.

After we left St. Petersburg, we had an exhibition game scheduled with the Cubs in Springfield, Illinois. Even though the game was rained out, it turned out to be an eventful day for the two teams. Dizzy was sold to the Cubs for $185,000, along with pitchers Curt Davis and Clyde Shoun and outfielder Tuck Stainback. Dizzy went around the clubhouse with farewells to the team, but when he got to me, he said, "I'm not saying good-bye to you. You'll be on the train tomorrow to Chicago." But, it wasn't meant to be. The Cardinals turned down the Cubs offer and Frisch named me as his rightfielder.

Opening Day in St. Louis was noted, not for being the first of 2,308 big league games that I would play in over the next 22 years, but as the first game that Medwick had missed since the Gas House Gang days, ending a streak of 485 consecutive games. He was replaced by Don Padgett, whom the Cardinals had used primarily as the rightfielder the year before, and who would become my roommate. With Medwick out because of the lumbago in his back, there were only five future Hall-of-Famers playing in that game. Along with Johnny Mize and myself on the Cardinals, the Pittsburg Pirates came to town with rightfielder Paul (Big Poison) Waner, his younger brother Lloyd (Little Poison) Waner and short-stop Arky Vaughan. Just for good measure, both of the managers in that game, Frisch for us and Pie Traynor for them, had retired as players the year before and were also future Hall-of-Famers. Much more significant to me that day was the fact that the Pirates had Johnny Rizzo, who had been my teammate the previous year at Columbus, starting in left field. St. Louis fans had an opportunity to compare their new rightfielder with the prospect the Cardinals let get away.

Big Poison got to us early that day, hitting a double and a triple. In the fifth, Padgett knocked in Don Gutteridge and Mize doubled in Stu Martin and Padgett to give us a 3-2 lead. Bob Weiland, our starter, held the Pirates from scoring any more until the ninth inning with two outs, when Rizzo singled again and Vaughan followed with a shot that I watched sail over my head to land on the roof of the right field pavilion, giving them the victory.

Despite the fact that I went three-for-five with a double, I didn't drive in or score any runs that game, while Rizzo accounted for two while going two-for-three.

After a while, Medwick was back in the lineup. He was a great ballplayer; you couldn't take that away from him. He was a bad ball hitter, although not quite as wild a swinger as Yogi Berra was later to become. You could pitch this righthanded hitter high and away and he could rattle the wall in right-center. With Dizzy traded away and Frisch through as a player, Medwick's presence in the lineup was the most visible link between my first Cardinal club and the Gas House Gang.

Medwick had a unique disposition. He tried to get in with the young guys when they first came up to the big leagues, but we soon shied away from him. He wanted to let you know that he was the star and if everything wasn't just the way he wanted it, he would be bitter about it. Eating out with him wasn't a whole lot of fun because he liked to show off and talk nasty to the waitresses.

As a manager, Frisch was something else. His personality did not reflect his Ivy League background, which had earned him the nickname, "The Fordham Flash." "Baseball is not a parlor game," he once said, and he didn't play or manage like that. He had earned a reputation as a hard-nosed player before the Cardinals gave up six-time batting champion Rogers Hornsby in order to get him from the Giants in 1927. Frisch didn't become playing manager himself at St. Louis until the 1933 season. After the Gas House Gang's triumph in 1934, Frisch cut down on his playing time until he retired in 1937 to concentrate on managing. He was tough. He had come up with the Giants under John McGraw. He didn't have the time or the disposition to take any nonsense from his players. If he told us to be at the ballpark at nine o'clock, he meant nine o'clock and not ten after. If you were late, he didn't want to hear any excuses.

Besides Medwick and Frisch, Pepper Martin, the Gas House Gang's third baseman, was still around, but by this time he was being used primarily as a utility outfielder. There will never be another Pepper Martin. He was the type of player who wouldn't let them wash his uniform if he had a good day. Back in those days, players wore the same uniform on the road that they did at home. Also, instead of these double-knit fabrics the players use today, we had those big wool uniforms. Pepper would play with nothing on under his uniform. No jock strap, no sweat socks, nothing. He didn't care how much he sweated in those hot things. If he was going good, he didn't want his uniform washed. The smell of victory in the clubhouse was not so sweet if Pepper was playing well.

Pepper could get the job done. He had broken into the regular Cardinals lineup as an outfielder in 1931 alongside an over-the-hill Ray Blades. When Medwick was promoted from Houston amid all the fanfare, Pepper was shifted to third base. He might not have had the softest hands at the hot corner, but if Pepper couldn't stop a grounder with his glove, he'd block it with his chest, his shoulder, or any other part of his body.

He led the National League in stolen bases three times and, although he never was much as a pinch-hitter, he always ended up with a high batting average, even after he became a part-time player.

When we went to Boston to play the Braves (or "Bees" as they were being called then), there was a pot-bellied, coalburning stove in the visitor's clubhouse. Martin offered to bet anybody that he could broad jump over that thing. Hell, he said he'd stand flat-footed and jump right over it. And he did, too.

One of his favorite pastimes was midget cars. In St. Louis, he'd play a ballgame in the afternoon and go out and race those midget cars at night. He also liked his beer, but he didn't want his wife Ruby to know about that. Ruby was a very religious woman and didn't approve of alcohol. If someone offered him a beer while we were at a party for the players and their wives, Pepper would slap it right out of his hand, saying, "You know I don't drink that stuff." But once he got out on the road, he'd be ready for a real night on the town.

Once, Frisch came up to Pepper before a game in Boston after he looked like he had a bad night, and told him he was playing third that day.

"Frisch, you didn't ask me if I wanted to play third," he replied.

"I don't care. Get out there. You're playing third," Frisch declared.

So Martin approached Bees manager Casey Stengel and said, "Casey, tell your guys not to bunt today because I'm playing third, and if they start bunting on me, I'm going to cause some trouble."

Sure enough, one of the Bees bunted. Pepper charged that ball and fired it right at the baserunner. The ball flew into our dugout, clearing the bench. Later in the game, their first baseman Elbie Fletcher was up to bat in a sacrifice situation. After he laid one down in Martin's direction, he ran to first, but instead of looking where he was running, his eye was on Pepper all the way down the line. Pepper again threw the ball right at him and the ball sailed into our dugout again, scattering everyone for a second time.

Other than Medwick, the only player in the lineup on a daily basis that year was first baseman Johnny Mize. His physical problems that spring carried on into the season, though, and he started off with a slump that had baseball experts dumbfounded. Finally, he started changing his stance. He got to changing it with each at-bat, and sometimes even with each pitch. His adjustments started to pay off, and, by the latter part of the season, he was right in there fighting for the batting championship. Mize was probably the best curveball hitter that I've ever seen. He was by then in his third season and had rapidly developed into a superstar.

As Mize was moving out of his slump, I started moving into mine. The pitchers started throwing me slow curves instead of the fastballs I had seen the first time around.

While Medwick and Mize were everyday players, everyone else was competing for playing time. Because I got off to a good start, I was the regular rightfielder at the beginning of the season, but when I went into a slump, I was benched for Padgett during the summer. Terry Moore and Pepper Martin shared centerfield duties during that season. Frisch played whoever was having a hot streak at the time.

I wasn't happy about being benched, but I wasn't ready to gripe about it. I was new to the big leagues, Frisch was a tough manager, and frankly I was scared. As a matter of fact, I hardly opened my mouth the first year I was with the Cardinals.

With "The Big Cat" at an early stage in his nine-life career, there didn't appear to be much of a future for my Columbus teammate Dick Siebert in the organization. At 26, he had nothing left to prove by playing in the minors, so the Cardinals sold him to the Philadelphia Athletics early in the season. From then until the end of World War II, he was Connie Mack's regular first baseman.

Other than Mize's corner at first base, the infield was also subject to quite a few lineup changes. Don Gutteridge, who had been the regular third baseman since 1936, switched over to shortstop to make room for Stripp. Later that summer when Joe was sent on to the Boston Bees, Gutteridge went back to third and the Cardinals brought up Lynn Myers to take over at short.

Stu Martin, another North Carolina boy, played more second base than anybody for us that season, while yet another Tarheel, Jimmy Brown, who had been the primary second baseman the year before, was the utility infielder, playing second, third, and short. The catchers, Mickey Owen and his backup Herb Bremer, had both come up to the Cardinals the previous year.

With Dizzy traded and his brother Paul injured, our pitching staff was in a state of transition. Southpaw Bob Weiland was our workhorse. For ten years, he had bounced around the American League without gaining much distinction. But, when he joined the Cardinals the previous year, Frisch used him so much that he ended up the season with more starts than anyone else, and seven relief appearances to boot.

With Dizzy gone, Lon Warneke was probably the best-known of the Cardinals pitchers that year. His fastball helped get him the nickname "The Arkansas Hummingbird." Warneke had come to the Cardinals with a better record than Weiland, having had three 20-or-more-win seasons for the Chicago Cubs. The Arkansas Hummingbird remained a winner during his years with the Cardinals, but he particularly helped me out, not on the mound, but with his bat. He noticed my discomfort in rightfield with ground balls that were hit to me, and decided he didn't want that fear in anyone fielding behind him. During that first year, he hit fungoes to me every day. Two or three would be fly balls, but the rest were grounders. This went on day in and day out, at home and on the road. I finally got to where ground balls were like anything else coming to me out there. Having mastered what I had once feared, I realized the importance of practice, practice, and more practice.

The Cards might have had Warneke much sooner except for an incident while he was pitching in the Cubs' farm system at Alexandria. Cardinal scout Charlie Barrett was in the Washington suburb to see if Lon was worth buying from the Chicago organization. In the fourth inning Lon hit a double, just before a sudden thunderstorm saturated the field. All the players scampered to their respective dugouts except for the fun-loving Arkansas boy, who remained at second base paddling an imaginary boat. The crowd roared in appreciation of his showmanship, but Barrett was unimpressed and reported that the pitcher was something of a flake. However, after he had won 100 games for the Cubs by age 27, the Cardinals decided that it was time for the tobacco-chewing righthander to join their flock. With a young Mize now established at first base, Gas House Gang first baseman Rip Collins was deemed expendable and traded to the Cubs along with established pitcher Roy "Tarzan" Parmelee for Warneke.

Curt Davis and Clyde "Hardrock" Shoun, the pitchers acquired from the Cubs for Dean, divided their time between starting and relief that year, as did "Fiddler Bill" McGee and Max Macon, who had moved up with me from Columbus. The Cardinals made other significant promotions to their pitching staff when they brought up Max Lanier and Mort Cooper near the end of the season.

I appreciate all the help Warneke gave me by hitting those grounders to help my fielding, but Terry Moore became my best friend on the club, and I would have to say that he was my best friend in baseball. As a rightfielder, I felt fortunate to have him play alongside me in centerfield. When I had to go back deep for a long fly ball, he would run to the wall and yell, "Careful!" if I was getting too close. He was the best defensive centerfielder I ever played alongside.

Someone else I got to know that year that I've remained friends with to this day is Gene Autry. The Singing Cowboy had always been a Cardinals fan; I met him in Pittsburgh, his home town, when we were there to play the Pirates. He visited us in the visitors' clubhouse at Forbes Field, and that night a bunch of us went to the rodeo to watch him ride his horse through a burning hoop. After that, I would go to see him whenever I was back home in Roxboro and he performed at the North Carolina State Fair in Raleigh. Because of him, I have a soft spot for his California Angels. He's been a terrific friend to me and has been great for baseball, and I sure hope the Angels win a championship for him some day.

Although my friendships with Moore and Autry have lasted over the years, my marriages have not. The beginning of the end of my first marriage came that summer when Hulo moved back to Roxboro.

1938 was the valley season of the Cardinal decline from the Gas House Gang's championship in 1934. The team had been going downhill each year for Frisch. In September, with the team in seventh place behind everyone but the hapless Philadelphia Phillies (who ended up winning only 45 games the whole season), Frisch was fired. There was some speculation that I had something to do with the manager's dismissal. Supposedly, Rickey had been against my being benched. Rickey and Frisch had words over this. As for me, I just kept my mouth shut that year and waited for my chance to get back into the lineup. And besides, those two had many more situations to argue about. When you're losing, it's easy to disagree. His replacement for the last 17 games, third base coach Mike Gonzales, knew his promotion was only temporary and he never stopped going to his third base coaching box each inning.

Dizzy won for the Cubs whenever he played that year, which wasn't very often, but that team got a lot of mileage out of Big Bill Lee, the league's best pitcher, and Clay Bryant, the strikeout leader. They won the pennant with the help of a home run by catcher-manager Gabby Hartnett at dusk one evening off Pittsburgh's ace reliever Mace Brown in Chicago's then-lightless Wrigley Field.

Until Hartnett's homer, Pittsburgh had given the Cubs a run for it. They had a tight infield led by shortstop Arky Vaughan, and a solid outfield with the Waner brothers and Johnny Rizzo. Rizzo played so well the St. Louis writers were complaining that the Cardinals should have sold me instead of him to the Pirates the previous fall. Rizzo batted .301 and was fifth in the league with 23 home runs. I ended up the season with only eight homers.

The offensive stars of our team that year were, of course, Medwick and Mize. Medwick, having dipped a bit after his Triple Crown season the year before, was still good enough to lead the league in runs-batted-in and doubles, while Mize led the league in triples and slugging average, and was second behind the Cincinnati Reds' Ernie Lombardi in batting average.

There seemed to be a professional jealousy between our two stars. They were both constantly fighting for the batting championship, and each would let an official scorer know if he felt he was being cheated by a play that was scored as an error. More harmonious was the relationship between Pepper Martin, Bill McGee, Bob Weiland, and Frenchie Bordagaray. Frenchie did a great job pinch-hitting for us that season. They had formed a jug band called the Mudcats. With Martin on guitar, McGee on fiddle, Weiland on the jug, and Frenchie on his damned washtub, they were quite a crowd favorite, even though Dizzy was no longer around and able to warble "The Wabash Cannonball" along with their playing.

Frisch, however, was not amused by their musical talents. He let them know in no uncertain terms that he was "tired of their Goddamned gittars and that silly jug and Frenchy's washboard" and that it was time to throw those instruments into the Manyunk River.

Once, shortly before Frisch was fired, we arrived in Rochester for an exhibition game with our top farm club. At the train station, we saw placards advertising the visit of our team. But the highlight of the ads were pictures of the Mudcats—with only small pictures of Medwick and Mize in the corners. Even though Frisch had told the band members to leave their instruments at the station, someone from the Rochester club, which had promoted the Mudcats, called the St. Louis office and arranged permission for the Mudcats to play. "We're supposed to be a ballclub, not a travelling circus," fumed Frisch. But the band played on. Over the winter, the Mudcats were able to draw like the devil at theaters and clubs, and they made good money doing it.

Speaking of trains and stations, 1938 was, of course, well before the days that teams traveled by jet. On our road trips, we took Pullman cars unless we had a short jump like going from New York to Boston. Then, we'd have private cars, but it wouldn't be a Pullman. Back in the early days, there were upper and lower bunks to sleep on for these overnight trips. Veterans slept on the bottom, and rookies slept up top.

These trains were supposed to be air-conditioned, but half of the time the air-conditioning wouldn't work. It seemed like every time we left St. Louis, it would be 105 degrees outside, and a lot hotter on the train if the air-conditioning wasn't working. On the more sweltering trips, Pepper Martin would pull the windows open so he could get some fresh air. Usually he ended up with a face full of coal smoke, his hand and shirt covered with smut.

Hotels weren't much better. There may have been some air-conditioned hotels in those days, but the Cardinals sure didn't stay in them. We'd have to settle for a ceiling fan.

No, it wasn't a plush existence. But, it was the major leagues. I'd have ridden a mule to the park, if necessary.

After Mike Gonzales took over for Frisch, I got hot in a series against the Reds. I went seven for 13 against Bucky Walters and Paul Derringer, Cincinnati's two best pitchers. Then we went to Chicago and I was benched. Maybe it was because Gonzales was afraid of catching heat for playing a rookie against a contending club. Also, it could have been that Branch Rickey was afraid that my batting average would keep going up and he would have to give me more of a raise than he wanted to pay.

For whatever reason, I sat out the final three games of my rookie season and I ended up batting .276 that year. It was a disappointment considering I had batted over 100 points higher in the American Association the year before, but, as it turned out, that was to be the lowest average I ever had as a Cardinal.

With a year of major league experience under my belt, I too was able to capitalize on the fact that I was a St. Louis Cardinal. I was offered a job with the General Grocery Company as a salesman for Manhattan Coffee. The money was better than I had been making as a cloth splitter for the mill, and it was quite a pleasant change of pace to be visiting with the restaurant and grocery buyers in the St. Louis area. In addition to Manhattan, I was also representing the Cardinals. My customers loved to talk baseball with me, and that was something I had been doing free for most of my life. The job was the beginning of an enjoyable association that lasted for years.

The part of my offseason spent back home in Roxboro turned out to be anything but enjoyable that winter. When I returned to our house on the family farm, I found that Hulo had moved back in with her own family. I didn't go to see her. As far as I'm concerned, there were no hard feelings. I was determined to be a major league ballplayer and remain in St. Louis, while life in that city with its heat and bustle just didn't suit her. We were destined to lead different lives and it was something that we just had to accept as we went our separate ways. Hulo and I would be divorced in 1941.

Right here might be a good spot to explain that, though I haven't looked it up, I'm probably close to the major league record in marriages and divorces. In the marriage column I'm 0-for-5, though the last one lasted 23 years, and I'm quite proud and happy my children have done so well. But as you might imagine, I've taken a lot of ribbing over the years as to my matrimonial problems. I'll be the first one to admit that sometimes I wasn't the perfect husband. On the other hand, sometimes things just don't work out like you hoped they would. Baseball, with all the travelling involved, is not always healthy for a relationship. Then too, in one sense, baseball has always been the consuming passion in my life; you might say I've always been married to baseball.

I can look back now on 1939 as the year that I became a major league star, but it was also one of the saddest years of my life and couldn't have gotten off to a worse start.

Between Christmas and New Year's, my father and I had gone rabbit hunting and bagged ourselves about twenty-five rabbits. I had just about finished cleaning all of them when he pitched in and helped. Pitching in to help had always been the way my father lived, and it turned out to be the way he died. He was helping me clean the rabbits when he cut his finger. A little cut on a finger seemed like nothing to a hand that had caught fastballs without a glove, so we didn't think anything about it at the time. But, those rabbits turned out to be infected with the deadly tularemia bacteria, commonly known as "rabbit fever."

My father took sick on New Year's Day, 1939. We took him to the hospital in Roxboro, but at the time nobody there knew anything about the disease. Finally, the local doctor got somebody over from a larger hospital in Durham, who told my mother that she had an awfully sick husband. Still, though, they couldn't do a thing for him. Four days later, his temperature went up to 107 degrees, and when the fever broke, he went with it.

While we were burying him, on top of my grief, I didn't know if I had rabbit fever myself or not. I found out a month later when I began to develop a kernel that grew to the size of a hen's egg under my left arm. Poison from the rabbit fever had produced a yellow streak all the way down that arm, and I couldn't straighten it out fully. I went to a country doctor, who started giving me some shots. I didn't notify the Cardinals about my illness. I figured that if they knew, I might not get a chance to make the team. My mother and Dr. Merrit urged me not to go to spring training, but my mind was made up. I received my final shot at Dr. Merrit's office at about five o'clock on a late February morning and headed straight for Raleigh, where I caught a train to the Cardinals spring training camp in St. Petersburg. For the next five months, I would still be unable to straighten out my arm.

3

For the first time since I had joined the St. Louis Cardinals organization, the team had a new manager in spring training. It was Ray Blades, a familiar face around the Cardinals' spring training camps. Blades and Rickey went all the way back to 1913. Rickey was in the American League managing the St. Louis Browns then and had agreed to serve as an umpire in the city's grade school championship baseball game. Ray Blades was an outfielder playing for the Franz Siegel School. He was just a little kid, but the former backstop couldn't help but appreciate the hell-bent-for-leather approach to the game that the lad demonstrated on the field. By the time Ray had finished high school, Branch had transferred to the National League. Rickey had become more than just the team's manager; he was also a general manager in the process of starting a revolutionary new practice in baseball: a farm system of minor league teams with players owned by the Cardinals.

Little Ray had joined the Cardinals farm system and rose up like a tornado through the ranks. His temper exploded at the opposing teams and, on occasion, at the Cardinals' front office. once, when he found out he was being sent back to the minors, he charged through the door of Mr. Rickey's office. He scattered the furniture and subjected the nonswearing Branch to enough profanity to last a battleship through a war. Another time, after he made the Cardinals in 1922, he got so mad that he ripped off his uniform.

Still, Branch liked this spark plug's competitive nature. Blades stood only 5'7" tall and weighed just over 160 pounds, but he kicked, scraped, and clawed his way into the Cardinals lineup.

For a few years, he was a fine leftfielder. His speed, drive and hard-nosed style of play made him an ideal leadoff man for the St. Louis club during the Roaring Twenties.

When second-bagger superstar Rogers Hornsby took over as manager, Blades' hitting really caught fire. In 1925, he hit .342 with 12 home runs for the Red Birds. He was almost as good the next year when the team won its first World Series. He might have gone on to be one of the great Cardinal outfielders if he had not collided with the concrete left field wall at Sportsman's Park during that 1926 championship season.

With a cracked kneecap, Blades looked like he was finished as a ballplayer, but Dr. Robert F. Hyland came to the rescue and sewed his knee back together. This was one of the revolutionary operations that made a breakthrough in what is known today as sports medicine. Dr. Hyland was team physician for both St. Louis clubs. His reputation was along the lines of what Dr. Frank Jobe's is today. Thanks to Dr. Hyland's surgical ingenuity, Blades stuck with the club as a part-time outfielder, pinch-hitter and holler guy on the bench until he was 36 years old.

When he hung up his spikes, he remained with the organization. He was managing at Columbus, Georgia, when the Cardinals first signed me. By the time I was assigned to that club, Blades had been promoted to Rochester, the Cardinals' Triple-A club. By the time Ray became my manager in St. Louis, he was 42, but still had the same fiery disposition.

Basically, Blades inherited the club that third base coach Gonzales had taken over from Frisch. Most noticeably absent was Frenchy Bordagaray, who had pinch-hit so well for us the previous season, but now was with Cincinnati. One bright spot on the roster was rookie Bob Bowman, a righthander from the West Virgina hills, who had bounced around the minor leagues for years.

We played the Yankees in six games that spring, with each of us winning three. The crosstown game that spring that stands out most in my mind is the slugfest at Waterfront Park where they beat us 12-7. I homered twice in that game, while Bill Dickey hit for the cycle. Joe DiMaggio had two doubles and a ground rule triple that rolled under the scoreboard. Everyone was hitting, especially for the Yankees. Lou Gehrig, however, went hitless in five trips.

Lou Gehrig was the highest-paid player in the game that spring. He was 35 at that time and already established in the record books as one of the great hitters. Even the last spring of his career, when he was a sick man, he impressed me by the way he could move. For a big man, he was really fast. But at the plate he seemed to have lost it. They were throwing strikes right by him.

No one knew that Gehrig was sick, because his illness had yet to be diagnosed. No one knew that I was sick because I didn't want to tell anybody. I knew that Ray Blades had made the Cardinals starting right field position my job to win or to lose. There were too many other outfielders around to admit something was physically wrong with me. So I didn't let anybody see the kernels under my arms, and no one noticed that I was unable to straighten out my left arm. I didn't let on that the real reason I wore sweatshirts was to fight the chill that was going on inside my body during those warm, sunny spring days in Florida.

Instead, I drew attention to myself with my bat. The day after I homered in the slugfest with the Yankees, I did it again in a game against the Dodgers. I was also hitting doubles and triples.

My showing that spring seemed to convince Cardinal management that I was ready to reach the potential I had shown in 1937. There was talk that I was ready to join Medwick and Mize among baseball's elite and give the Cardinal lineup a one-two-three punch.

Medwick and Mize had established themselves as being among the best hitters in baseball, and wanted to be paid accordingly. And that was damn near impossible to do in St. Louis during the '30s and '40s. Despite their accomplishments on the field, the Cardinals had to stress the stars' shortcomings in order to avoid the salaries being paid to the New York 'name' players. Medwick and Mize had been at or near the top of most National League hitting categories for several years and, while they didn't have as many home runs as Gehrig or DiMaggio, they both had higher batting averages than the two Yankee greats during that period. But when it came to salary, the Yankee stars were light years away from our guys. While Gehrig was signed to a $43,000 contract and DiMaggio made $35,000 in 1939, both Medwick and Mize had to settle for less than $20,000.

Medwick took the situation particularly hard. Here was a man who really believed in striving to make all the money he could. In 1938, he had followed up his Triple Crown season by leading the National League in RBI's and in doubles (for the fourth consecutive time), as well as placing second in total bases and third in slugging percentage. His batting average, while a respectable fourth among the league leaders that year, was 52 points below what he had hit for the Cardinals in that incredible 1937 season. As a result, Medwick's salary was cut $2,000. That didn't set well with Muscles, who held out well into spring training and, I believe, carried the grudge against the team all season. It was widely speculated that he wanted to move on to Brooklyn, where he could command a larger salary and also be with Leo Durocher, his friend from the Gas House Gang days.

Mize, on the other hand, arrived in St. Petersburg not only on time, but also slimmer than the previous year. He had worked out daily during the off-season at the Missouri Athletic Association and was set to get off to a good start in the batting race. Even though he had led the league in total bases and slugging the previous season, he meant to claim the batting title instead of settling for second as he had the previous two seasons. He felt that the aches and pains he had suffered during the early part of the past season had cost him the title, and he was determined not to let that happen again.

As for me, I was not bothered by my annual salary of $3,300, a fraction of what these stars were making. Maybe I wasn't very smart to accept the paltry salary Rickey offered me. I never could get anywhere trying to negotiate with him. He would throw big words at me until I was glad to sign my contract just so I could get out of his office. I just wanted to prove that I belonged in the major leagues and that I could help the Cardinals win.

Once again, we opened our season against the Pirates, except that we played at Forbes Field, and we won. Their righty Bob Klinger had us down 2-0 in the top of the seventh, when Medwick singled to score Little Jimmy Brown and Don Gutteridge, and to drive me to third. Mize then flied to Rizzo in shallow left field. Taking a chance against Rizzo's arm, I tagged up and hustled to the plate, beating his throw to score the winning run.

That play may have symbolized the crossing of my career and Johnny Rizzo's. After the Pirate outfielder's exceptional rookie season, which inspired some of the St. Louis sportswriters to speculate that I should have been sold by the Cardinals instead of him, his career started going downhill and that talk died down.

Another deal that started to look good for the Cardinals that year was the Dizzy Dean trade. When Big Bob Weiland came down with a sore arm, Curt Davis replaced him as the workhorse of our pitching staff. It seemed there was nothing Davis couldn't do in 1939. He became a big winner for us as a starter, and also finished some crucial victories for us in relief. Furthermore, he did a lot of damage for us at the plate that year.

Meanwhile, things just weren't going that well for Diz. His sore arm kept him on the disabled list a lot but, unlike in 1938, he was not as effective in his rare appearances. Following his trade to the Cubs, he didn't make his first start in St. Louis until June 18, 1939, well over a year after the deal.

Besides Davis, another former Cub was having a better year on the mound for us than Dizzy was having. The last week in April, Lon Warneke shut out his old teammates twice. On April 29, during the second of those two whitewashes, the Arkansas Hummingbird had a no-hitter going in the top of the seventh at Wrigley Field when Stan Hack hit a weak roller by him that Mize fielded. Lanky Lon dropped the first baseman's toss, and the Cubs' third baseman was given credit for Chicago's only hit that day. It's always nice when a pitcher gets as many hits for you as he gives up, and Warneke did just that in that game. He also kept hitting me those grounders in practice.

Actually, back then all of the guys on the pitching staff got some starts and also helped out in relief. Bowman, the 28-year-old rookie, started fifteen games and still found time to lead the league in saves, with nine. Of course, nine saves today wouldn't even lead a club, much less the National League. But back then, nobody cared how many "saves" a pitcher had. There wasn't even such a term in baseball as "saves." If Blades had wanted to run up Bowman's total, he wouldn't have started him fifteen times. But we were impressed that he won seven games coming out of the bullpen without a loss, and that his ERA for the year was a scant 2.60.

Offensively, Pepper Martin got off to the hottest start. As a fourth outfielder, and also as Don Gutteridge's backup at third, Pepper was hitting as he had never hit before. Not only that, but he was a great baserunner. On May 8, he ruined a great performance by Dodger righthander Red Evans. In the top of the sixth, in a scoreless tie at Ebbets Field between Weiland and Evans, Pepper led off with a single, advanced to second on an infield grounder by Medwick and on to third on another roller by Mize. Then, as Evans stood on the mound and wondered how he could keep Terry Moore from driving Pepper in, Martin suddenly darted for the plate. Evans just stared in shock with his mouth open as Pepper scored the only run of the game.

The end of May found the old Wild Hoss leading the National League with a .382 batting average. This was good news for us on the field, but it meant bad news in the clubhouse. Remember, Pepper wouldn't allow the attendants to wash his uniform if he was playing well. During a hot streak, I'd swear that uniform could stand up by itself.

Despite the odor of his uniform, Pepper was a favorite of teammates and fans alike. After an old wrist injury slowed him down, the club held a "Pepper Martin Day" for him on June 18 of that year. Sportsmans Park looked more like a barnyard that day as the Hoss was given a couple of strawberry roan brood mares, a sow and a litter of pigs, and a plow. The plow was compliments of his hometown friends from Oklahoma City, and was presented by fellow Okie Carl Hubbell, who happened to be in town with the visiting New York Giants.

"Get 'em good and fat," Lon Warneke told Pepper of the pigs (a team gift) that we were bestowing. "We're all coming down to your farm next winter for a good ham dinner."

I think ballclubs were knitted together much closer back then than they are today. When teams were on the road, it wasn't unusual to see five, six or maybe ten guys on a team sitting together and talking. Being around each other on those long train rides really developed a spirit of camaraderie on most clubs back then. When we were on the road and playing night games, normally a bunch of us would gather about 11:30 in the morning at our hotel and go to a movie. We'd get out around two in the afternoon, come back to the hotel to eat and rest for a while, then be ready to go to the ballpark. You don't see a cluster of travelling ballplayers around the lobbies of their hotel like you used to. You might see one guy here with his lawyer, and another player over there with his agent, but today very rarely is a team's presence felt much around a hotel.

It makes me feel a little sad when I go to oldtimers' games and dress with other former players in a room connected to the clubhouse of the home team. One or two of the modern players might go out to watch us play before their game, but most of them seem to prefer to stay in their lounge and listen to music.

Anyway, back to 1939.

At the age of 28, Dizzy Dean was a legend, but his career had peaked and he was on what turned out to be a rapid downslide. After being the workhorse of the National League in the first five seasons of his career with the Cardinals, Diz had been hit in the elbow by a line drive off the bat of Cleveland Indians outfielder Earl Averill while pitching in the 1937 All-Star game. When his turn to pitch for the Cardinals came in Boston, he told Frisch he was ready. It now looks like coming back from the All-Star game injury too soon made his arm turn bad. He pitched well in limited action for the pennant-winning Cubs of 1938, but in 1939 his luck was starting to run out.

Paul Dean was also down on his luck in 1939. He failed to win a single game for us that season, his last with the Cardinals. Paul had never been the same since he injured his arm during spring training in 1936. Paul always blamed that injury on the fact that he had thrown too hard that spring before he had a chance to get in the proper condition. By the time I was up with St. Louis, it appeared Paul was always afraid he was going to hurt his arm again, and consequently timid to really cut loose. On May 15, Paul (who, by the way, we never called Daffy) won his last game as a Cardinal. Unfortunately, it was against the University of Illinois during an exhibition game in Champaign. Tom McConnell, a St. Louis boy who never reached the major leagues, homered off him. Pepper Martin came in to pitch the last inning for us and held them scoreless.

While all the Cardinals hated to see Paul losing it, at least we had the improvement of Bill McGee to cheer us up. Fiddler Bill won his first four decisions that year, the fourth on June 1 in a 1-0 shutout over the Giants. 1939 was also the year that Mort Cooper started to raise some eybrows. He started off the season with some great relief pitching and soon became a part of the starting rotation.

One of Weiland's last victories was against another old master, Carl Hubbell, in mid-July. Hubbell hadn't started in six weeks at the time, and, even though I didn't get a hit off him that day, Pepper, Terry, and Don Gutteridge were enough behind the relief pitching of Big Bob and Mort to beat him.

A lesser-known Giants pitcher gave me much more trouble than Hubbel. My first four years in the game, New York had the biggest man in baseball pitching for them. Righthander Jumbo Brown was a former American Leaguer who was at the end of his major league career when I came up. The Giants were an appropriate team for him to play for because Jumbo stood 6'4" and weighed almost 300 pounds. His age and his weight must have affected his stamina, because he couldn't pitch for many innings at a time. But, used by his manager strictly as a reliever, Brown was a very difficult pitcher to hit. He was a short-arm pitcher, and could really fool the hitters. It seemed like every time we played the Giants and a clutch situation came up, manager Bill Terry would bring in Jumbo. Brown got me out better than any other pitcher in baseball. For many years, Bill enjoyed reminding me of how difficult that journeyman reliever was on me.

The home runs I had hit in spring training didn't come once the season started. Not being able to straighten out my arm until

July took its toll on my ability to hit for power, and my first homer was delayed until June 27. That homer was doubly satisfying because it won the game for Lon Warneke over his old Cub teammates, and raised his record to 9-2.

I was glad to be of help to Lon. The Arkansas Hummingbird had really boosted my confidence as an outfielder with all those fungoes he had hit me. That year, instead of dreading ground balls, I was much more aggressive in right field. I went after everything, and it showed in the stats. I led the league in putouts, assists and double plays for an outfielder. But there was still more work to do on my defense; I also led the league's outfielders in errors.

The Cubs had lost their magic of 1938. Hartnett again started his workhorse Big Bill Lee more than any other National League pitcher, but the 6'3" righthander just wasn't as effective as he had been in previous years. Third baseman Stan Hack led the league in steals again with 17, but his .298 average meant an off year for him and wasn't enough to carry the club to contention. They finished fourth that year, 13 games out.

The team to beat that year was Cincinnati. Their first baseman Frank McCormick was entering his prime, leading the league in hits for the second year in a row and becoming the league leader in runs-batted-in. Another offensive star for them that year was catcher Ernie Lombardi, who challenged Mize for the home run title. They also had great pitching from Bucky Walters and Paul Derringer, whom they had picked up six years earlier from the Cardinals in the deal for Leo Durocher.

People like to talk about how Charlie Finley tried to get orange baseballs approved for major league play when he owned the Oakland Athletics in the 1970s. Well, in 1939, there were actually yellow baseballs used in a few regulation games. Some professor had claimed that they were easier to see. I remember we used yellow balls in the first game of a double-header with the Dodgers. I guess I didn't see it too well because I made an error, and southpaw Vito Tamulis held me hitless.

In July, as Pepper Martin started to cool off, Mize's bat really got hot. He took over the home run lead from Ernie Lombardi.

Johnny Mize was, without a doubt, one of the best curveball hitters I've ever seen. A pitcher could throw our first baseman his best breaking ball and the Big Cat would rip it right out of the ballpark. What a great swing he had! It gave him the rare ability to be both a great power hitter and a good contact hitter. That combination also resulted in the highest slugging average in the National League during the first three years I was up. He might not have been Fancy Dan at first base, but he was better than some I've seen playing over there. Besides, he sure did drive in the runs for us.

Too bad he wasn't being well paid for it. I've said it was tough for a ballplayer to make any money in St. Louis, when we had two major league teams in town. The Cardinals did well to draw 350,000 fans in an entire season back in those days. Our American League counterpart, the St. Louis Browns, had established themselves by then as perennial also-rans, and were drawing less than we were. But they still had their following. There just weren't enough people in the area to support ballplayers who wanted to make the top dollar. That's why guys like Mize and Medwick became disheartened playing in St. Louis, and wanted to move on to New York where there was more money to be made.

Once the season got underway, we all started thinking about money. World Series money, that is. On May 10, we advanced to a tie for first with the Cincinnati Reds as three hits apiece off righthander Claude Passeau by Brown and Medwick enabled Warneke to gain a victory over the Phillies at Shibe Park. With no batter able to hit ten homers and only one pitcher, Kirby Higbe, able to win 10 games, the "Futile Phillies," as they were called that year, ended up dead last, winning only 45 games.

We took sole possession of first the next day as the Reds were nosed out by the Dodgers. The following night, we gave them a rude homecoming at Crosley Field by scoring five times in the fifth with the help of the first of Mize's two circuit clouts in the game. It was the first defeat of the year for Paul Derringer, who, by that time, had earned three victories. At the time, we did not realize that Derringer, whom the Cardinals had traded away for

Leo Durocher during the 1933 season, was to actually improve his winning percentage for the 1939 season from that point.

The next night, we were losing 2-1 to Johnny Vander Meer with two out in the ninth, when I came up to face the southpaw with Don Gutteridge on first. I doubled to center, but Harry Craft, who earlier had knocked in the go-ahead run, nailed our third baseman at the plate to end the ballgame.

Despite the fact that Gutteridge failed to outrun Craft's throw, he was considered to be one of the fastest players at that time. There was even talk early that season of having him race Washington Senators outfielder George Case during the All-Star break to determine the sprinting championship of the major leagues.

During a series in May, Reds pitching had held me to two doubles in 12 at-bats, but another boy from North Carolina was looking good in defeat. Our lead off hitter Jimmy Brown had gone 7-for-17 with three doubles and a triple, and accounted for nine of our runs during that four game series by scoring five and driving in four more. Though he stood less than 5'9" tall and weighed only 165 pounds, Little Jimmy was really a scrapper. In fact, Eddie Dyer was known to have told anybody who wanted to know that Brown, whom he had managed while with the old Greensboro (N.C.) Patriots during Jimmy's first year out of N.C. State, was the scrappiest competitor he ever managed. When trouble hitting curveballs from lefthanders was hampering his advancement in the organization, Brown became a switch hitter in midgame, and later became a .300-hitting major leaguer.

Something else had happened which made Brown more valuable to the Cardinals. After Creepy Crespi and Joe Orengo both made errors at shortstop during a 6-3 loss at the hands of the Giants, Blades moved Brown from second base to shortstop and let him play there every day. Although he had been used at second and third quite frequently throughout his professional career, Jimmy always maintained that he preferred playing shortstop. Installing him at that position filled the void evident on the club since Durocher had been traded to the Dodgers. By the beginning of the 1939 season, Brown had a history of arm problems, attributed to his tendency of being overly anxious to get rid of a ground ball he fielded. At St. Petersburg, the Cardinals, in order to relax his delivery style, ordered him to count to three after fielding a ball before he threw to first. As a result, his throws, while still powerful for such a little guy, did not cause his arm any pain.

Losing three out of four at home, as well as first place to the Reds, seemed to have knocked the wind out of our sails as we followed our seven-game winning streak in late May with a June swoon. But, ironically, as I look back, that was the period in which I really established myself as a major league star. Until then, I had not really lived up to the advance billing generated by such a great season at Columbus in 1937. My rookie year got off to a good enough start, but I slumped that summer. In early '39 I was frequently sitting out in favor of a hot Pepper Martin. But then during a two-week period I raised my batting average 25 points. Pittsburgh followed Cincinnati into Sportsmans Park and took us two out of three, while I went 7 for 12 at the plate. I drove in four runs in the third game with three doubles, but my old Columbus, Ohio roommate stole the show as Rizzo drove in an incredible nine runs with two homers, two singles and a double as we blew a 7-1 lead to give the Pirates a 14-8 victory.

We started out the month of June by dropping two of three to Bill Terry's Giants at the Polo Grounds. In the rubber match of that series, we had a one-run lead with a man on in the top of the seventh when Curt Davis, our workhorse, was brought in to face Tony Lazzeri. For 12 years, which included the glory days of Ruth and Gehrig in their prime, Lazzeri had been the second baseman for the New York Yankees. By this time, however, old "Poosh 'Em Up" was finishing his career as a part-time third baseman for the Giants. Still, there was some life in his bat, as he drove in the tying and winning runs by belting Curt's pitch into the left field stands.

The Brooklyn Dodgers was a team on its way up. Shortstop Durocher had replaced Burleigh Grimes as manager at the beginning of the season and was molding his own personality onto the club. Dolf Camilli, a free swinger, was their primary run producer, as well as a top-notch defensive first baseman. Third baseman Cookie Lavagetto had what it took to get on base and to keep the pitchers nervous after he did.

Still, the Dodgers didn't really contend that year and the pennant race came down to the Cards and the Reds. For a stretch in September, Cincinnati was hot, winning 16 our of their last 20. Still, they lost ground on us, as we won 18 out of our last 21. I was red hot during that streak. My rookie jitters were behind me. So was my rabbit fever. I felt that there was nothing that could stop me now.

I wasn't in awe of the big shots on the club anymore. In fact, the way I was contributing to the success of the ballclub, I considered myself to be among them. No more hiding in the background for me. I'd probably have to say that 1939 was the year that Enos Slaughter's personality was established once and for all.

At that point, we went to Cincinnati, needing to win three games out of four for the pennant. We only took two, so Cincinnati went to the World Series. When Derringer pitched the flag-clinching game against us, it marked the first time the Reds had won the Senior Circuit title since the 1919 club that beat Shoeless Joe Jackson and his infamous group of Chicago White Sox.

Twenty years after the Black Sox scandal, the Reds weren't so lucky. The Yankees beat them four straight to sweep the Series.

Sure, I was disappointed about not being in the World Series after we had come so close. Still, I was satisfied that I had established myself as a major league star. I had batted .320 and led the league in doubles with 52. The fans in St. Louis were really starting to appreciate me, and it sure was a great feeling. It was to be a long love affair.

4

We went into 1940 feeling like the Cardinals were going to be the National League's team of the decade. We really felt that we were a young club very much on the rise.

It seemed like there were always loads of young outfielders coming up from the farm system. At one time, there were as many as 800 players in the Cardinals system. Despite the abundance of minor league teams, most of the Cardinal farm clubs held their own, and we always had quite a few championships below the major league level.

Because of the caliber of players challenging me for my job each spring, I realized from the beginning that if you weren't in shape to play the game, you wouldn't get very far. I always made sure I did plenty of running in the offseason to keep my legs in shape. For anyone who wants to play baseball, keeping your legs in shape should be first priority. I found that your arm will always come around when you keep your legs and body in shape.

Mr. Breadon was pleased with the young talent in the system, but mad as hell over what some felt was Medwick's lackadaisical play at the end of the previous season. He cut Joe's salary down to $18,500. Muscles was enraged and insulted. He had hit .332 and driven in 117 runs, and felt besides that he had been underpaid all along. The star outfielder stormed out of spring training camp, but Breadon still wouldn't budge.

"It's sign on my terms or else," the Cardinals owner insisted, and the way things were set up back then, Joe didn't have any choice but to return to camp and accept the cut. It was obvious to all by then that his days as a Cardinal were numbered.

Shortstop Marty Marion came up to the Cardinals that spring. He was a lanky boy from South Carolina. At 6'2", he was the tallest shortstop in baseball at the time, even though he weighed only 170 pounds. The press liked calling him "Slats," but most of us on the team referred to him as "the Octopus." His long arms, with his ability to move in all directions, gave the Cardinals stability at shortstop for the first time since Durocher had been sent to the Reds. Marion went on to become the team's everyday player at that position for many seasons. Though younger than I, he would someday become my manager on the Cardinals. And, twenty years after our first spring together, he would help get me signed as player-manager for the Chicago Cubs top farm team.

When the Cardinals originally offered Marion a professional contract, he wouldn't sign unless they also signed an Atlanta boy by the name of Johnny Echols. Echols actually beat his friend to the big leagues, getting into a couple of games for us as a pinch-runner late in the 1939 season, but after that, he never played in the majors again. Also beating Marty to the majors was his older brother Red, a longtime minor league outfielder whose major league career consisted of a total of 28 games for the Washington Senators.

Some of our optimism was dampened during spring training when Curt Davis took sick and Jimmy Brown and Johnny Mize came down with knee problems. Once the season got started, the injury problems grew even worse. Medwick started off like he had in 1938, missing the first 10 games with a bad back. Marion ruptured a ligament in his knee. Brown's knee got better, but then his nose was broken.

But the biggest problem for the Cardinals was the pitching staff. Bob Bowman had a sore side, Mort Cooper had a sore arm, and the whole staff was just plain sore about the way the hurlers were being shuffled around by Blades. We gave up a lot of runs early that season.

I guess you could say I was carrying the team because I started the season the way I ended the previous one—with a hot bat. Too bad I wasn't carrying it very far. We were closer to last place than we were to first. One of my biggest boosters around the league

was none other than Frank Frisch. My rookie year manager had
spent 1939 observing National League action as a radio commentator for the Boston Bees before replacing Pie Traynor as the manager at Pittsburgh. "Slaughter is one of the greatest kids to come
into the league in years," said the former Cardinal skipper. "He
got off to a bad start the one year I had him, but he made up for it
last season, and this spring he's even better."

He may have benched me some during my rookie year, but
the Fordham Flash remained a booster of mine for the rest of his
life.

For what it was worth, another fellow that helped us early in
the season was Joe Orengo, a 26-year-old rookie. With both
Brown and Marion hurting, the San Francisco native was a handy
man on the ballclub because he could play second, third and short.
And like me, he started the season batting well over .300.

In fact, the versatile infielder had a nine-game hitting streak
in May. It was snapped when our entire team was held to one hit
(a single by Stu Martin) in Cincinnati on May 26. That game was
played in only one hour and 37 minutes. The Reds that day were
officially raising the pennant that they had won in 1939 on their
flagpole. They were on their way to a second consecutive National
League title. In the stands were Judge Landis, the Commissioner
of Baseball, and 21 longtime baseball fans who in 1869 had actually witnessed the Cincinnati Red Stockings play in the very first
professional game in what has become our national pastime.

By Memorial Day, the Cardinals were in seventh place, ahead
of only the Phillies, and rumors were flying around like buzzards
over a dead body. Joe Medwick was said to be on his way to Cincinnati for outfielder Harry Craft and shortstop Billy Myers. That
wasn't true. Ducky was headed elsewhere. And Branch Rickey
was rumored to be on the verge of firing Blades. Our general manager issued a statement denying this. And he didn't fire Blades.
Breadon did.

The beginning of night baseball in St. Louis marked the end
of Ray Blades' career as the Cardinals manager. Twenty-three
thousand fans came to see us face the hated Dodgers on this land-
mark occasion, and Durocher's team pounded out ten runs to our

one, scoring five times in the first. The crowd didn't take the one-sided nature of this game lightheartedly. Their booing was punctuated with bottles hurled onto the field.

Blades was canned on June 7. Having seen Frisch let go less than two years earlier, I started to realize that managerial change was in the nature of baseball. Third base coach Mike Gonzales was once again named to take over as interim manager, but very soon it was announced that Billy Southworth, who had been managing at Rochester, would take over.

Another big change sent Medwick to the Dodgers along with Curt Davis, in exchange for outfielder Ernie Koy, third baseman Bert Haas and pitchers Carl Doyle and Sam Nayhem. Koy, who succeeded Medwick in left, helped us with his bat the rest of the season, and Nahm helped some on the mound the next, but that was about all we got out of that foursome. Doyle pitched his way out of the majors that same season, while Haas, who two years later would resurface with Cincinnati, never made our big league club. The key to the deal was that four letter word Breadon and Rickey always went after in big trades: C-A-S-H. It was believed to be somewhere around $130,000.

Anyway, Medwick had finally been able to rejoin his pal Durocher. Muscles might have been popular with Leo the Lip, but sentiment for him was not particularly high on the team he left behind. A lot of the players thought he had shortlegged us a bit during the pennant race with Cincinnati at the end of the 1939 season. He didn't appear to be playing as hard as he had earlier, when he was in the race for a batting title. His efforts in left field were particularly suspect. One night late in the season, he played a ball hit his way so poorly that Blades sent another fielder out there to replace him before the next pitch was thrown.

Heated words were exchanged in the clubhouse following the game. Blades was upset with the moody slugger for loafing in the outfield. Medwick was incensed with the manager for showing him up. A few days later, it was announced that the differences between the two had been patched up, but Medwick's presence seemed to bring out more and more ill feelings on the team.

Joe's relationship with Terry Moore had seriously deteriorated after an incident in the outfield. Joe and Terry had been playing alongside each other in the Cardinals outfield for six years when a ball was hit high and deep into left center. As Terry went charging toward the fence in pursuit, he relied on Medwick to warn him if he were in any danger. Medwick was hollering that Moore had plenty of room as the ball sailed 20 feet into the stands. Terry crashed into the concrete wall. When he came to, Moore told Medwick that if he ever ran him into the fence again, he'd break Joe's neck.

This and other not-so-pleasant events lingered in the minds of many of Joe's ex-teammates. The fact that he now wore a Dodger uniform made him an even more obvious target of Cardinal wrath.

A few days after the trade, we headed for Brooklyn to take on Medwick and his new teammates. We checked into the New Yorker where, it turns out, both Medwick and Durocher had been staying. Taking the elevator down to head for the ballpark, the Dodger duo found themselves sharing it with Bob Bowman, who was scheduled to pitch for us that day. Anything that had resembled a friendship between Bowman and Medwick had disappeared the previous season when Bowman had accused Joe of lackadaisical play in the outfield. For that matter, Bob didn't think too much of Leo either, so it should be no surprise that the conversation among the three ballplayers was somewhat less than pleasant.

If you haven't had a chance to review the sworn testimony, or if you haven't read Leo's book *Nice Guys Finish Last,* Durocher started the conversation by insinuating that his club would send Bowman to an early shower that day. Bowman then replied by saying that he felt he was talking to the one automatic out he could always count on in the Dodger lineup. Medwick interjected at that point, telling Bowman he wouldn't last long enough to get a chance to face Durocher.

Once the game got started, each of the first three Dodgers greeted Bowman with a base hit. It turned out that third base coach Charlie Dressen, who had an uncanny ability to steal signs, noticed that Bowman was twisting his glove whenever he threw a curve ball. Then Don Padgett, who was catching for us that day, noticed that Dressen was whistling every time Bowman threw a curve. With Medwick coming up to bat, Padgett went to the mound and told Bowman to hold the glove the way he did when he was throwing curves, but to fire a fastball in high and tight.

Up came Medwick. When he heard Dressen's whistle, he leaned towards the plate and rared back in anticipation of belting a predetected curve. Pow! Bowman's fastball caught him right on the temple, and he dropped to the ground like a stone. Out like a light.

That's when all hell broke loose. The Dodgers charged at Bowman like a mass of hornets. They were not only led by manager Leo Durocher, but general manager Lee MacPhail. From right field, I rushed to the mound in aid of Bowman, along with the rest of the Cardinals. When I reached the scene of the melée, I grabbed the first Dodger I could reach, which happened to be Van Lingle Mungo. I had Mungo by the hair and my arm was around his neck when Freddie Fitzsimmons came along and collared me. Terry Moore jumped in and, in turn, collared Freddie.

The story didn't end with the free-for-all. MacPhail, incensed over the damage done to his brand new six-figure investment, tried to get Bowman banned permanently from baseball. He even took the case to the New York district attorney, but Medwick, from his hospital room, was ready for the whole thing to be dropped. It was.

Nothing against Blades, but I had to have good feelings about working under Southworth again. He had saved my career during my first spring training by telling me to run on my toes instead of flat-footed.

Southworth was like a father to me. His considerate and courteous nature was a boost to the morale around a clubhouse that had been on edge under the rule of the fiery Blades. Billy took over a club with a 15-29 record and led it to 69 victories in the next 109 games.

Most people thought we would slip some in our offensive production from left field. Koy, who had been the Dodgers leftfielder, was batting only .229 at the time of the Medwick trade, but the third-year major leaguer, who was already in his thirties, went on to hit .310 for us that season. Our offense slipped—but from right field. I started an eastern road trip batting a lofty .371, but by the time we returned I was all the way down to .216. I was able to get only three hits in 82 at-bats over that stretch. Fortunately, back home, I snapped out of the slump and rebounded, finally finishing the season with a .306 average.

Cincinnati again won the National League pennant that year, this time by a comfortable 12 games over the Dodgers. Once again Bucky Walters led the league in wins (22) and ERA (2.48) and they also got another 20-game season out of Paul Derringer.

Thanks to the .633 winning percentage we posted under Southworth, we ended up at 84-69, good enough for third. With a strong finish, we left the year feeling as we had during spring training—excited about our chances for a pennant in the near future.

5

By this time, the Cardinals were feeling good enough about Mort's brother Walker to pick up some more bucks from their sugar daddies in New York. The Dodgers had gotten some good years out of a good-hitting catcher named Babe Phelps. The 6'2", 225 pound Phelps, also nicknamed "Blimp," was starting to show wear and tear. Their backup catcher Gus Mancuso was traded to us in exchange for Mickey Owen. The Dodgers also threw in John Pintar, a pitching prospect who never quite made it to the big time. And, oh yes, Brooklyn sent along a little cash, this time about $60,000 worth.

1941 turned out to be one of the most frustrating seasons in the history of the St. Louis Cardinals. Just as the team was about to really come together, injuries tore it apart. We had a great lineup. Too bad the position players in the starting lineup for us on opening day only played together for a grand total of four games the entire season.

Walker Cooper had the first serious injury. Our promising rookie was making his mark in the National League when he came down with a separated shoulder diving to nail a baserunner at home. Later Mancuso was hit by a pitch, and Don Padgett was lost to us. Frank Crespi lost considerable playing time in' 41. First he dislocated a finger and then got hit in the face by a line drive. Jimmy Brown was also lost for a spell due to a broken hand, causing a further weakening of the infield.

Even though our team was decimated by injuries, we were the only National league team to give the mighty Dodgers a run for their money in that pennant race. The Lords of Flatbush went

on to collect 100 victories that year, three more than our flock of
bad-winged Cardinals.

At 34, Dolf Camilli had his best season that year as he led the
league in home runs (34) and runs-batted-in (120). Though he was
12 years younger than Camilli, Pete Reiser also had what turned
out to be a career year. The original "Pistol Pete" won the batting
championship with a .343 average and led the league in runs, doubles and triples. The budding superstar would eventually see his
career seriously curtailed by injuries, but 1941 was his year to play
and the Cardinals' year to nurse wounds and wonder about what
could have been.

One dream did come through for this St. Louis Cardinal that
year. I finally got into an All-Star Game. The contest was held in
Briggs Stadium in Detroit, home of the Tigers. I wasn't the starting
rightfielder for the National League. That honor went to Bill Nicholson of the Cubs. And he was replaced not by me, but by the
Pirates' Bob Elliot, who was converted to third base the following
year. Cincinnati manager Bill McKechnie sent me in to bat for
Elliot in the seventh. I got a base hit off Washington's Sid Hudson.
When Pittsburgh's Arky Vaughan followed with a home run, our
league took the lead.

Unfortunately, the ecstasy of the moment didn't last. Ted Williams had botched up my single, allowing me to take second base,
but the Boston Red Sox outfielder had the last laugh that day. In
the bottom of the ninth with two out, two on and his league a run
behind, Williams drove a ball in my direction. No, I didn't botch
it up. I just watched it sail deep into the stands.

As I hustled off the field, I could see Ted jumping, clapping
his hands and laughing out loud as he circled the bases. He had
plenty to be happy about. Not only had he won the All-Star Game,
but he went on to hit .406 that year, and no one in the major leagues
has hit over .400 since.

There was one thing I had that Williams didn't that year,
though—a team in a pennant race. Ted's Red Sox finished 17
games behind the mighty New York Yankees in 1941. Despite all
our injuries, the Cardinals stayed neck and neck with the Dodgers
all season long. That's what made the season so frustrating. If we

had stayed healthy, I'm sure we could have finished far ahead of Brooklyn.

By August 10, I had driven in 71 runs, second in the league only to Bill Nicholson. But that day, it was my turn to go down. We were playing the Pirates at Sportsmans Park when Stu Martin, who had been sold by Breadon to Pittsburgh the previous December, drove a ball to right center. Terry and I were both chasing after it. At the last second, I saw Terry dive for the ball and snare it with a spectacular catch. I tried to jump over him, but I didn't quite make it. I was slammed to the ground on my left shoulder.

When I looked up, there were Southworth and Moore staring down at me. "Are you okay, Eno?" my manager inquired.

I assured him that I was, but I guess he didn't believe me. As we walked together back to the dugout, we both believed there was nothing seriously wrong, but when our team physician examined me after the game, it turned out that my collarbone was broken. I spent the next two weeks in St. John's hospital. There, Dr. Hyland wired my shoulder back together.

Terry remained in one piece after that accident, but he wasn't so lucky a few days later, when his head was in the way of a pitch thrown by Boston's Art "Lefty" Johnson. That left our outfield in the hands of Coaker Triplett and Estel Crabtree, aging veterans who in recent years had been playing in the minors.

Ernie Koy was gone early in the season for Pep Young of Jamestown, North Carolina. Young, the Pirates third baseman in the late '30s, was by then a fading utility infielder. He ended up playing six games for us that year, three as a pinch-hitter. That was the last of his major league career except for 27 games for the Cardinals at the height of the World War II depletion of talent in 1945.

With a rapidly-thinning outfield, it was time for the Cardinals to pick up an outfielder from Rochester that Rickey had originally signed as a pitcher. Up came a left handed hitter named Stanley Frank Musial. Though he hadn't turned 21, the Pennsylvania Polish boy, who was in the process of becoming "Stan the Man," went on to hit .426 for us for the last six weeks of the season. The Cardinals wisely decided to let him stay for awhile.

Another Polish kid from Pennsylvania joined us from Rochester late that year. George Kurowski, who went by the nickname "Whitey," went on to solve our third base puzzle.

Creating even more excitement at the time were two pitchers named Howard, brought up from Houston. The first of the two Howies had actually been with us before, appearing in eight games in 1937 and 1938. But righthander Howie "Spud" Krist didn't jell in the big leagues until he was 25 years old and won ten games for St. Louis without a loss during the 1941 season.

The other Howie, surname Pollett, started off the season making a name for himself at Houston as he won twenty games while losing only three, with an equally amazing ERA of 1.16. The left-handed Cajun boy from New Orleans continued to mystify opposing hitters even after he was promoted to the National League. He took up where he had left off in Houston, pitching nine games for us at the end of the season, winning five with two shutouts.

It was a knockdown, dragout race all the way that year. We jumped out front with the Dodgers, and our two teams left the rest of the National League out of contention. At one point, both of our clubs had winning percentages of over .700. We held the lead for most of May and June, but by the Fourth of July, injuries were taking their toll on us, and it was the Dodgers who were spending most of the time on top. We did manage to pull two games ahead by July 24, but by August, Brooklyn had passed us again. Throughout the month of August, our two clubs were seldom more than a game apart. With a September push, they pulled ahead again and won the pennant by 2 1/2 games, but we lasted until the final weekend of the season.

The excitement we created on the field drew 646,000 fans to Cardinals games at Sportsmans Park that year, the most since 1928. Of course, that figure was dwarfed by the Dodgers and the Giants. The wealthier New York teams had a double advantage over smaller market teams like the two that shared St. Louis. They could afford to buy the top name players from their less-affluent counterparts, who always seemed to be looking for ways to raise more cash. Also, they could afford to pay their stars better.

Like Medwick earlier, Mize was disenchanted playing in St. Louis, and he was starting to look East where the money was. Finally, after the season, the Cardinals would accommodate him and he would join the Giants.

I felt very much on the sidelines. The Dodgers took on their crosstown rivals, the Yankees, in that World Series. No other American League team had come close to the Yankees that year. And neither did the Dodgers.

Joe DiMaggio had made history by hitting in 56 straight games that year. Dodger pitching kept him relatively tame with a .263 average, but no Dodger regular hit higher than Medwick's .235 as Brooklyn dropped four games out of five to the Bronx Bombers.

Forced to watch on the sidelines, we Cardinals wondered how we would have done against the Yankees if all our players were healthy. In 1942, we would find out.

My goal that winter was to rehabilitate my shoulder. Instead of traveling for Manhattan Coffee, I stayed in St. Louis and worked in a jewelry store. I waited on the ladies and had a lot of fun. Sold quite a bit of jewelry, too.

Staying in St. Louis, I got to rehabilitate my shoulder at the Missouri Athletic Club. Even though I was able to get in a little playing time at the end of the season, my shoulder had a long way to go. As late as Christmas, I could hardly raise my left arm. And there were still pieces of bone coming up through the skin, some of them big as peas.

I started going out to the athletic club three times a week. There, I tossed large, heavy medicine balls, pulled weights from a pulley, worked out on a rowing machine and played some volleyball.

That doesn't mean I didn't do any traveling. In December, I made a personal appearance for the Cardinals in Peoria, Illinois. There, for the first time, I met Jack Brickhouse, who was then with a radio station in Peoria. Brickhouse was, of course, later to become the voice of the Chicago Cubs and is now in the broadcaster's wing of the Hall of Fame. But, at the time, I was more excited about meeting the young piano player at our hotel.

She was a Chicago girl named Josephine Begonia, and it was her 15-piece orchestra that was playing there. We became friends that weekend and a serious item in a hurry. We would get married in 1943.

I must have been in a better frame of mind after meeting Josephine. My shoulder started getting better, and all that working out must have had my whole body in better shape than ever. When it was time to head for my annual pre-spring training visit to Roxboro, I was trimmer than ever at 178 pounds. In previous seasons, I weighed no less than 185 pounds, and that was in the heat of the summer.

As a ballplayer, I always did what I felt kept me in the best physical condition. In those days, I never drank alcohol. I didn't really have anything against it. In fact, now that I no longer play, I do take drinks on occasion. Even though I've been in the tobacco all my life, I've never smoked. In fact, back then, I didn't chew either. I had tried some chewing tobacco that we had just cured when I was a youngster, and it made me sick. That stuff out of a barn is awfully strong.

6

In March of 1942, the Cardinals assembled in St. Petersburg for spring training. With the departure of Mize, the last of the big money players was gone. And while John was able to get his wish to make bigger money with the Giants, those of us left with the Cardinals were all young, lean and hungry. We averaged only 26 years of age. I don't think I was ever as proud to be with a ballclub as I was to be one of the 1942 St. Louis Cardinals. I've played with other great clubs, but I would have to say that this one topped them all.

The amazing thing about our club was that it was able to win so much despite selling off star after star. When players like Dizzy Dean, Joe Medwick, Mickey Owen or Johnny Mize were bartered away to teams in larger cities, you can bet a significant amount of cash also exchanged hands, and that it was Sam Breadon's hands ending up with the greenbacks. Trades, if you could call them that, of that nature showed up more in the club's bank account than they did on the roster.

Another thing Breadon had done to make some greenbacks was accept an endorsement from a vitamin company. What did the players on the team get out of the deal? Free vitamins. That 1941 season when the team stayed in the pennant race all year despite all of the injuries, it was written by some that we were being inspired by vitamins.

Now don't get me wrong, I believe in vitamins. I still take them every day. In fact, later on in my career, I had my own contract with a vitamin company. But what made the Cardinals special was that we were a team of players who always felt we could win. No matter how far we were down, or regardless of who had been sold or injured, we always thought that we could beat anybody.

Our first spring training game of the year confirmed those feelings. We beat the mighty Yankees 4-2. Scores aren't that important in a spring training game, but as we left their camp at crosstown Waterfront Park, we felt that if our players could collect twenty hits to their three, then we were a better team than they were.

Of the three players acquired in the Mize deal, only reserve catcher Ken O'Dea stuck with the club for more than five games. And O'Dea was originally a product of the Cardinals farm system. First baseman Johnny McCarthy was included in the deal. He had been the Giant regular at that position for a couple of years before the acquisition of Zeke Bonura turned him into the team's pinch-hitter. McCarthy didn't even make our club in spring training. Pitcher Bill Lohrman, the third man acquired, did, but after five appearances for us the righthander from Brooklyn was shipped back to the Giants along with catcher Gus Mancuso, who was unhappy in his role as backup. By the time Mancuso returned to St. Louis nine years later, he was Harry Caray's color man in the radio booth.

Anyway, despite the fact that recent big-name Cardinals were now playing in different uniforms, the Cardinals roster was still composed primarily of players who had been brought up through Branch Rickey's extended farm system. All of the everyday players came up through the ranks and all of the front line pitchers with the exception of Gunboat Gumbert were also homegrown boys. Well, Lon Warneke wasn't raised in the Cardinal organization either, but by July, he had been sold back to the Cubs. And southpaw reliever Clyde Shoun, whom Rickey had obtained four years previously in the Dizzy Dean trade, was sold to Cincinnati after pitching for us in two games.

Another transaction of note, as far as I'm concerned, was the sale of my roommate Don "Red" Padgett to Brooklyn for $20,000. Red was to spend the next four seasons wearing U.S. Navy blue instead of Dodger blue. The apparent loss of green made Brooklyn general manager Larry McPhail see red. He tried to get his club's money back, but Commissioner Kennesaw Mountain Landis allowed Breadon to keep the funds he had acquired for the catcher-outfielder.

Even without Padgett, the Dodgers were quite a formidable team. They quickly jumped out in front of the pack. Frankie Frisch's Pittsburgh Pirates pulled within a half game of Brooklyn by May 4, but Durocher's boys proceeded to win 11 out of 12, leaving the rest of the league behind in a trail of dust.

At that point, there was talk that Breadon and Rickey had sold the hopes of a pennant for St. Louis down the Mississippi River, but Cardinal executives pointed to Ray Sanders, a local softball player, who went on to work his way up through his hometown team's farm system. Sanders was rated a better fielder than Mize, and had really been hitting at the two Columbus farm clubs.

The lefthanded hitting Sanders may have lived up to his advance billing as a gloveman, but at the plate, he found National League pitching quite a bit more difficult to hit than that from the American Association. He batted only .252 with five home runs for us that year—not much offensive production from the first base spot in the lineup. As the season progressed, Southworth went more and more with Johnny Hopp at that position. "Hippity" had succeeded Joe Medwick in left for us the year before, only to be squeezed out of the outfield later in that season by the emergence of Musial.

Another change in the regular lineup that season put Whitey Kurowski at third base. Kurowski was a unique individual, and as a player was different from just about anyone else who has ever played pro baseball.

Back when he was an eight-year-old child growing up in Reading, George Kurowski severely gashed his arm when he toppled off a fence and landed on some broken glass. His father, not realizing the potential danger of the situation, failed to take his injured son to a doctor. Not until two years later, anyway, when the boy's arm became so racked with pain that it needed to be checked out. It was discovered that osteomyelitis had set in and had actually rotted part of the bone away in his right forearm. Even though Whitey possessed one of the strongest arms in baseball, three inches of bone was missing from it. Team physician Dr. Hyland thought it was a miracle that he could throw at all, much less harder than most major league infielders.

With Kurowski added to the lineup, Jimmy Brown, at 32 the elder statesman on the club, moved to second. That put Frank Crespi on the bench. Though only 24, "Creepy" was in the final season of his major league career. Only shortstop Marty Marion kept his starting infield position for the entire year. Slats also went on to outlast the new infield starters and several of their successors. By the time Solly Hemus took over his position in 1951, Marion was the manager who gave the new shortstop his assignment.

In his first full season as our regular catcher, Walker Cooper was establishing himself as one of the premier backstops in the National League. Though his major league career was just starting, the strapping 6'3", 210-pounder had been through seven minor league seasons, and was anything but intimidated by his National League competition. Crouching behind the plate, he enjoyed chewing his tobacco and seemed to take a special pleasure out of depositing the excess juice on an opposing hitter's shoes. When he did this, the batter would step out of the box with a scornful stare at our juice-spitting catcher.

"Well, what are you going to do about it?" Coop would ask as he crouched down there, tough as an oak and wearing a chest protector to boot. I'll tell you what they did about it: nothing.

Walker and Mort Cooper were without a doubt the best "brother battery combination" in history. Walker did a great job for us that year, but the way Mort pitched in 1942, his brother could have been a lousy catcher and they still would have made a great combination. At 29, the elder Cooper was having his best season in baseball. His overpowering fastball combined with a breaking forkball proved to be too much for the hitters to handle. And he was at his best against the stronger clubs, especially the Dodgers, whom he beat five times with only one loss.

While Mort was replacing Lon Warneke as the top dog of our pitching staff that year, the man who made the Arkansas Hummingbird expendable was Johnny Beazley. The righthander from

Nashville, Tennessee, had finally made it to the big time after spending five tough years in the Cardinal farm system. He pitched for us that year like he was going to spend a long time in the major leagues. He probably would have had it not been for an arm injury in World War II.

Another guy besides Mort who was at his best against the Dodgers was Max Lanier. This Tarheel lefty was 5-2 against Brooklyn, which won 104 games that year, but only 8-6 against the rest of the league in 1942. Throughout his 12 seasons as a teammate of mine in St. Louis, Max always seemed to put a whammy on the Dodgers.

It's hard to put your finger on why we seemed to do so well against the Dodgers. We wanted to beat everybody, but if there was only one team we could beat, it would have been them. The cocky confidence of Durocher and Dressen made them a team everybody in the league loved to hate. Now that it's all over, and I've had more time to look at everything in perspective, I do have to admit one thing: I think I really would have enjoyed playing for Leo Durocher. He was a hell-bent-for-leather type of manager, who wanted the same type of player. He liked to see hustle in his ballplayers, and I liked to see the same thing from my teammates.

Harry Gumbert started 19 games for us and relieved in 19 others. Gunboat, whom we had picked up from the Giants in a trade for Bill McGee early in the previous season, was the most active of the 1942 Cardinals not brought up through the team's farm system. The only other member of that squad that didn't have a Cardinals upbringing was reserve catcher Ken O'Dea, another ex-Giant.

Besides Gumbert, our pitching staff went deep with fellows who could both start and relieve. Howie Pollet spent his first full season with us and, in addition to starting 13 games, he relieved in 14. That was the most he was used out of the bullpen until the twilight of his career in the mid-fifties. Ernie White, another lefty, wasn't the workhorse he had been the year before when he exploded on the scene, but he still was able to win some key games for us.

While Pollet and White were not quite the pitchers they had been the year before, Howie Krist was, and more. Having won all 10 decisions in 1941, he went to 16-0 for the two year period before he finally got beat. He was the best reliever on our staff that year and, with eight wins from the bullpen, led the National League. He was also good enough to win five more in eight starts.

The most significant rookie pitcher for us that year was a righthander from Missouri named Murry Dickson. Dickson was another who could both start and relieve. He could pitch a complete game and relieve the next day. He had a rubber arm and was ready to go at all times.

A great relief staff like the one we had on that team makes it hard for me to buy the argument that hitters have lower averages today due to the fact that relief pitchers were not of the quality they are today. I'll put a bullpen composed of guys like Howie Krist, Murry Dickson, Harry Gumbert, Howie Pollet and Ernie Whitt, at least the way they were in 1942, against any major league team's bullpen today.

Perhaps modesty should prevent me from expressing my pride in the Cardinals outfield that year but, what the hell, this is my autobiography, and I am damned proud to have been a part of that outfield. Musial, Moore, and Slaughter. I truly believe that all three of us belong in the Hall of Fame.

Musial, the youngest, went on to become the first of us to be enshrined at Cooperstown; 1942 was his first full season and proved to the National League that he was going to be around for a while.

Terry Moore had, of course, established himself in center for us, but I've said it before and I'll say it again: defensively, he is, without a doubt, the greatest centerfielder I ever played alongside. For that matter, he was the best I've ever seen. I'm not the only former teammate to say that he deserves to be in the Hall of Fame on account of his defense alone. Terry, as I also mentioned earlier, was my best friend in baseball. He and I began sharing hotel rooms while the team was on the road that year after Padgett had been sold to Brooklyn. We remained roommates until he retired as a player.

Anyway, all modesty aside, I'm proud to say that the three of us made quite an outfield that year. We didn't mind getting our uniforms dirty if it meant robbing opposing batters of base hits. "No outfielder ever closed the gaps on a line drive with more élan than the Musial-Moore-Slaughter trio," wrote Donald Honig in his book *Baseball's 10 Greatest Teams.* While Musial was establishing himself as one of the league's top hitters, I was leading the Cardinals that year in most of the batting categories, including average, hits, triples and home runs. Enos Slaughter leading a championship team in home runs? Yes, that's exactly what happened in 1942. How many did I hit? A grand total of thirteen. And that's two more than I needed to lead the club, because Musial was next with only 10.

That's not to say that home runs were that difficult to hit in the summer of '42. Mel Ott, who by this time had replaced Bill Terry as the Giant manager, led the league in home runs again, this time with thirty. His first baseman, Johnny Mize, the slugger we had dealt to the Giants over the previous winter, hit twice as many as I did. And having two of the best power hitters was enough to net the Giants third place that year.

Home runs don't always mean victories. It turned out that Ott's first year as manager was to be the best of his seven year career at the helm of the Giants. Once Mel started to lose his batting stroke, it became harder and harder for his teams to win. As the talented and gracious outfielder's playing career slipped deeper and deeper into its twilight, opposing National League pitchers discovered they could throw the ball towards the left-handed slugger's elevated right foot and get him out. As it turned out, 1942 was his last great season as a slugger. But in '42 when Mel was still hitting them out, there were still too many weak spots on his club for the Giants to contend.

The team to beat, once again, was the Brooklyn Dodgers, who were making a run for their second consecutive NL pennant. Oh, how we wanted to beat those Dodgers! I can't think of a better feeling I've had than watching the last out in a game in which we beat the Dodgers; I can't think of a worse feeling than watching the last out in a game in which the Dodgers beat us. We played hard against everybody. But the adrenalin just flowed harder when we played them.

The antagonistic behavior of Durocher and Dressen, on and off the field, made the team easy targets for our wrath. Another thing the Cardinals held against the Dodgers was the fact that while all of our regulars were homegrown, none of their everyday players were. Cardinal starters were proud that we had all come up through the team's own minor league organization. Now, don't get me wrong. This doesn't mean that I hold anything against a player who has played for different teams. Hell, I moved around a bit myself later in my career, but in 1942, we always were looking to come up with a new way to despise Leo and his boys.

For starters, Joe Medwick, Mickey Owen, Curt Davis, Pete Reiser and manager Leo Durocher had come to the Dodgers courtesy of our own Sam Breadon. Their first baseman Dolf Camilli had been rescued from the lowly Philadelphia Phillies. The rest of the infield was manned by future Hall-of-Famers. Recent acquisitions Billy Herman and Arky Vaughan added to their already illustrious careers in 1942. Herman, whom MacPhail had picked up from the Cubs the previous midseason, immediately improved the club. Vaughan, after spending the previous ten years as the solid-hitting, slick-fielding Pirate shortstop, was switched to third, replacing Cookie Lavagetto.

Unlike Herman and Vaughan, who each had only one good year left for Brooklyn following 1942, Pee Wee Reese was at the beginning of his Hall of Fame career. A farm hand in the Red Sox organization, he had displayed great potential. But Boston manager Joe Cronin was not ready to give up the starting shortstop position he still occupied. Meanwhile, Brooklyn's shortstop-manager Durocher was more than happy to step aside as a starter in favor of a youngster with long range promise. It is interesting to note that during Reese's 16-year career with the Dodgers, Brooklyn appeared in seven World Series while the Red Sox only made it once.

Their left fielder Medwick is another member of the '42 Dodgers who is in the Hall of Fame. Like Herman and Vaughan, he is enshrined at Cooperstown primarily for what he had accomplished before joining the Dodgers. Muscles was only 30 years old that season, but his home run output had declined considerably since his days with the Cardinals. The man who had tied Ott for the home run lead in 1937 with 31 could only come up with four of them in '42. He still displayed some pop in his bat by batting .300 with 37 doubles, but his relationship with his former pal Durocher was rapidly cooling off and, by early the following season, Ducky was sold across town to the Giants.

Brooklyn's centerfielder Pete Reiser also came up through the Cardinals organization, but that's about all he had in common with Medwick. This was one hustling ballplayer. Having led the league in hitting the year before, he looked like he was on his way to do it again, when he took off like a bat out of hell after a fly ball I had hit in a game against them in July. Remember, they played hard against us, too, and "Pistol Pete" played hard against everybody. This time, it backfired on him. He would have won the race to the ball if the fence hadn't been right there at the finish line. As he crashed into the concrete wall at Sportsmans Park, the ball popped out of his glove. He was stunned for a few moments, long enough for me to clear all the bases for an inside-the-park homer. It added insult to injury against Reiser. Serious injury, I'm sorry to say. Even though he was back in the lineup six days later, he complained of headaches. The budding superstar was never the same ballplayer again.

The Dodgers had been fortunate to pick up Dixie Walker from the Detroit Tigers during the 1939 season. And I'll just note that their catcher was our ex, Mickey Owen, and move on to the Dodgers pitching staff that year.

It, too, was led by refugees from other clubs. Whitlow Wyatt came from the Cleveland Indians while Kirby Higbe came from the Phillies. We had sent them Curt Davis along with Medwick. Larry French and their relief ace Hugh Casey came from the Cubs.

While Padgett joined the Navy instead of the Dodgers after Brooklyn had purchased his contract from us, another former roommate, Johnny Rizzo, played in 78 games for Brooklyn, the most of any substitute. The outfielder many had said the Cardinals should have kept instead of me in 1938 was with his fifth National

League organization in five years and also was in his last major league season.

Anyway, like them or not, they were a damned good team, good enough to jump out in front of the pack at the beginning of the season. Actually, Pirate manager Frankie Frisch got his team off to a pretty good start also. On May 2, the Bucs, with players like Jimmy Wasdell and Pete Coscarart replacing guys like Paul Waner and Arkie Vaughan, were just a half game behind Brooklyn. Then Leo's boys went on a tear, winning 11 out of 12, and the Pirate ship sank into the second division.

By August 10, the Dodgers were ahead of us as well, by ten full games. At that point, we started to pull together and play like the team that we knew we were. The next couple of months have to be the period I enjoyed best in baseball. We were 43-8 during the last 51 games of the season. We might not have had the home run hitters, but we were hitting everything else. We led the league in total bases, as well as doubles and triples. We were never afraid to take the extra base. Furthermore, there was a closeness on that team that I truly believe has been unmatched in modern times. Once we got rolling down the stretch, we felt we just couldn't be beat. Unlike the well-paid Dodgers, who, in most cases, had already established themselves elsewhere, we were young, lean and hungry. The regulars had only played for one team, the Cardinals. And none of us had been on the Gas House Gang team that won the Series eight years earlier. But we just *had* to have that post-season money, and more importantly, that post-season pride.

Larry MacPhail must have noticed just such an air of determination about us. He called a team meeting with his Dodgers in the middle of August and, though they still were sitting on a comfortable lead, he told the team flat out that they were going to lose the pennant. Rightfielder Dixie Walker, beloved by the Brooklyn fans who referred to him as "The People's Cherce," offered to bet his general manager a couple of C-notes that his Dodgers were going to win. Naturally, MacPhail didn't take his outfielder up on the wager, but think about it: The ballplayer was attempting to bet on baseball. He wanted to bet on his own team. Was he kicked out? Hell, no, he wasn't. He played for nine more years, until he was 39. He also continued in the game as a coach. I'm not saying he shouldn't have. I just thought I'd mention it.

The name "Bums" was an informal moniker of the Brooklyn team started by a cartoonist named Willard Mullin. Much less remembered is the name he tried to pin on us, the St. Louis Swifties. Rather than the hobo he used to symbolize the Brooklyn players, Mullin's drawing depicted a riverboat gambler. Now, St. Louis is, of course, located on the Mississippi River and we did win games with speed, but the nickname didn't stick in the fans' hearts like "Bums" did in Dodgertown. I think it was because the image of a slick, deceitful card shark was not at all what our style of play was all about. We worked hard and gave a total, honest effort for every run we scored and for every opponent's run we stopped. We were just playing good old country hardball.

In addition to being called "swifties," we were being compared to everything from jackrabbits to a track team. But we had more going for us than speed alone. We had the best pitching in the league. Mort Cooper and Johnny Beazley finished first and second in the league in both wins and ERA. When Cooper was pitching, he would wear the number of the victory he was trying for that day. We didn't mind switching numbers with him like that. We did hope we would only have to give up our number for that one game. The way he was pitching, that's the way it usually happened.

We won 21 out of 25 in September, while the Dodgers, who lost five games in a row at mid-month in the only slump of their season, finished with a flourish by winning their last eight games. We won our last six, enough to beat them by two. We had racked up 106 victories that season, the most for a National League club since the 1909 Pirates. With 104 wins, the defeated Dodgers had set a record for a team finishing second.

I guess the odds must have been about ten-to-one against us going into the World Series against the mighty New York Yankees. Names like Joe DiMaggio, Red Ruffing, Bill Dickey, Lefty Gomez, Phil Rizzuto and Tommy Henrich help explain why they won 103 games that year, ten more than Boston (though the Red Sox had Triple Crown winner Ted Williams). Their World Series record was even more formidable. Since 1927, New York had won all eight of the World Series they had participated in. While winning those 32 World Series games, they had lost only four.

At first, the oddsmakers looked right. Red Ruffing came to Sportsmans Park and made history by becoming the first pitcher to win seven World Series games. For a while, he was really making it look easy. He had a no-hitter going against us in the bottom of the eighth with two out. Finally, Terry Moore singled to right, but he was left stranded.

Meanwhile, the Bronx Bombers had shellshocked our ace. Mort Cooper may have been the best pitcher in the National League that year, but the Yankees had knocked him out in the eighth and by the bottom of the ninth, they were humiliating us 7-0.

With a man on and two out in the bottom of the ninth, Ruffing issued a walk to Ray Sanders. That turned out to be the turning point of the Series. Marty Marion drove in our first two runs of the Series with a triple, and backup catcher Ken O'Dea singled him in. When Jimmy Brown followed with another base hit, Yankee skipper Joe McCarthy brought in Spud Chandler, a mound ace, who had gone 16-8 during the season. This time, we didn't play dead at the sight of another top-notch Yankee hurler. Terry Moore and I both singled. By now, four runs were in, the bases were loaded, and at the plate Stan Musial represented the tying run. He grounded to first, ending the game, but we left the field filled with confidence rather than humiliated by defeat. In the clubhouse, the mood was one of optimism instead of disappointment. That ninth inning rally may not have been enough to win the battle, but it was enough to give us the feeling that we had what it took to win the war.

The next day, Southworth put our righthanded rookie sensation Johnny Beazley up against Ernie Bonham, who had also had a great season in 1942. It was a contest between two 21-game winners who were having career years. We jumped out early, but an eighth inning, three-run homer by Charlie Keller put them back in the game. In the bottom of the eighth, I doubled and, as I slid into second base, I also slid into Phil Rizzuto. The Yankee short-stop bobbled the ball, enabling me to take third. I was able to score the go-ahead run when Musial hit a three-and-two pitch from Bonham into centerfield for a base hit. In the ninth, I gunned down my former Cardinal teammate Tuck Stainback as he attempted to take third, killing the Yankee rally and giving us our first Series victory.

Two days later, our southpaw Ernie White pitched the game of his life against Spud Chandler. What a masterful game Ernie pitched for us that day! His arm was so numb, he said he wouldn't have felt anything if somebody had stuck a fork in it. He might not have had feeling in his arm, but he had enough to shut out the Yankees in a World Series game for the first time since Jesse "Pop" Haines had done it for the Cardinals in 1926. Chandler didn't do too badly himself, giving up only a run in the third. Actually, the Yankees surrendered that run by winning an argument with the umpire. Kurowski had walked and Marion bunted him to second. McCarthy and his catcher Bill Dickey raised so much hell, arguing that Marion had bunted foul, that umpire George Barr sent him back to the batter's box. Slats responded with an infield single, once again moving Whitey to second, but this time with nobody out. White then bunted him to third, and he scored as Brown grounded out. We were happy to take the run, and it was all we needed, but there were times when it didn't look like it was going to hold up. With one on in the sixth, Joe DiMaggio lined a shot to center which Terry Moore managed to nab by leaping sideways. In the seventh, New York second baseman Joe Gordon hit one off White that was headed to the left field stands, but Musial saved a run with a leaping catch. Then, after we had scored an insurance run off Marv "Baby Face" Breuer, there were two on and two out in the bottom of the ninth when Charlie Keller hit a ball to the right field stands deeper than Gordon's fly had gone to left. I went back to the wall and, as I was jumping as high as my legs would propel me, a fan threw an orange out of the stands. Fortunately, I caught the ball instead of the orange and White's shutout was preserved.

The next day, Sunday, October 4, a record crowd of 69,902 showed up at Yankee Stadium for the fourth game. Our ace Cooper was going against Hank Borowy, a rookie righthander who had dazzled the American League that year with a 15-4 record. We knocked the New Jersey boy out in the fourth inning by scoring six runs, enough to give Mort a five run lead. But the Yankees caught up with us in the sixth, with the aid of a three-run homer by Charlie Keller. Still, though, the team remained unfazed by the fact that its top pitcher had been knocked out of the box. In the seventh, we went ahead to stay off Atley Donald, a lefthander from Morton, Mississippi, with the nickname of Swampy. Max Lanier held the Yanks scoreless for us for the final three innings and was credited with the 9-6 victory.

The grand finale came the next day, when Beazely was brought back to face Ruffing. Phil Rizzuto hit Beazley's first pitch into the left field seats. I tied it for us by hitting one off Ruffing in the fourth. New York scored again in their half of the inning, but we closed the gap once again in the sixth. Finally, in the ninth, Walker Cooper got a base hit and Whitey Kurowski, who had been hitting long foul balls all day, drove a Ruffing pitch into the left field stands a few feet to the right of the foul line. Going into the bottom of the ninth with a 4-2 lead, Beazley gave up a base hit to Yankee second baseman Joe Gordon and Bill Dickey reached on a grounder to second that Jimmy Brown bobbled. With the tying runs on base, none out and Jerry Priddy at the plate, Walker Cooper suddenly knocked the wind out of their sails by firing the ball to Marion, who tagged out Gordon. The decibel level from the home-team fans dropped sharply at that point and remained low as Priddy popped out and Yankee veteran George "Twinkletoes" Selkirk came to bat as a pinch-hitter. In 1935 Selkirk had succeeded Babe Ruth as the Yankees rightfielder, but now the 34-year-old Canadian was making his final appearance in the major leagues. Once again, a grounder was hit to our second baseman. This time, Brown handled it flawlessly. We had dethroned the mighty Yankees as World Champions.

That was a happy moment for me for obvious reasons, but it was a sad one, too, for I had already enlisted in the armed forces. World War II was raging, and I didn't know when, if ever, I would get to play professional baseball again. I was 26 years old. By the time I eventually returned to the Cardinals, I would be almost thirty.

7

Though I had enlisted in the Air Force on August 27, 1942, I wasn't called into service until the following January 23. I reported to what is now Lackland Air Force Base in San Antonio, Texas, for the purpose of attending preflight school.

Things didn't work out for me at the Cadet Aviation Center in San Antonio like they had at World War I Memorial Stadium in Greensboro. The doctors at the base decided that I was color blind, and they told me that I would have to find another way than I had expected to serve Uncle Sam.

Since I was grounded, I expected to be shipped out. In fact, I had my bags packed. But the night before I was supposed to leave Lackland Air Force Base, orders came from the Eighth Service Command to keep me in San Antonio.

I stayed there for the next two years as a physical training instructor for Squadron 43-J. My job as a sergeant was to make sure that the boys in my squadron were in top physical condition. All the spring training and pregame drills that I had participated in with the Cardinals turned out to be perfect experience for my new job.

But the real reason I stayed at Lackland was the formation of the eight-team San Antonio Service League. I spent 1943 as the right fielder for the San Antonio Aviation Cadet Center Warhawks. My manager was Lt. Del Wilber, who was also the team's catcher. Del, in fact, had been playing in the minor leagues for the Cardinals. He would later become a teammate of mine in St. Louis.

Joining Del and me before the year was out would be another Cardinal, Howard Pollet. The rubber-armed Texan had the best ERA in the National League before he traded in his Cardinal wings for those of a Warhawk.

The Service League games were played at a ballpark called Tech Field, which was also the home of the minor league San Antonio Missions. On the whole, it wasn't major league pitching that I faced in that league, but I did go up against some guys who would have been major leaguers if it hadn't been for the war. Tex Hughson had gone 22-6 the previous year for the Boston Red Sox. The year after the war, both he and Bob Ferris were to be 20-game winners for Boston, but at this time, they were both facing me in the Service League. So was Clint Hartung, who was to go on to pitch for the Giants.

Just because most of the players didn't have names that were in the national sports pages didn't mean that I didn't have to give it all I had on that field. Some of the major leaguers, I understand, played conservatively, so that they wouldn't injure themselves and jeopardize their future, but I didn't see things that way. Just as I had ever since Eddie Dyer had scolded me in 1935 at Columbus, Georgia, I ran to and from my position in right field. Del and I both felt that we needed to be examples for our teammates. We hustled all the time and expected the rest of the Warhawks to do the same.

It worked. SAACC (the abbreviation as it appeared on our uniforms) won the Service League championship title that year, and I won the batting title, hitting .498.

I got to attend the World Series that year as a guest of the Cardinals. Southworth had led the team to a pennant by 18 games against the second place Cincinnati Reds. Musial, moving over to my old spot in right field, was the batting champion and MVP. He also led the league in doubles and in triples.

The first of June, the Cardinals had used Coaker Triplett in a trade to get Danny Litwhiler to take over in left field. Although Pollet may have been the league's best pitcher that year until he joined us in the Air Force, Mort Cooper was, once again, the National League's big winner with 21 victories. His brother Walker hadn't done badly behind the plate, either. But, even with this wealth of talent, and to my disappointment, the Yankees won the World Series over the Cards that year in only five games.

The next year, I slipped a bit and only hit .419. But I enjoyed playing in that service league. According to the San Antonio sportswriters, my constant hustle made me a favorite of the fans at the park.

After two years in San Antonio, I was called upon by Lee MacPhail, now in the army himself, to join a group of former major league ballplayers on a tour for our troops in the Far East. MacPhail was upset that the Navy team had been beating up on the Air Force team in Honolulu, so he called for ballplayers to come to the aid of the morale of Air Force cadets all over the world.

The former Reds and Dodgers general manager rounded up 46 players in all. We originally met in Kerns, Utah. After training there, we headed to Seattle, and from there we shipped out to Honolulu. Right after we arrived in Hawaii, however, the Navy team disbanded, so we were never able to play them.

We were then divided into two squads. I was assigned to a team stationed at a park called Hickham Field. My teammates included second baseman Joe Gordon from the Yankees and catcher Birdie Tebbetts of the Detroit Tigers. Tebbetts had played against me in the San Antonio Service League.

Also on that team training at Hickham were shortstop Billy Hitchcock, also from the Tigers, Don Lang, a former Cincinnati Red who would later play third base for the Cardinals, and, once again, Howard Pollet.

We spent 1944 playing ball in Hawaii against a team that trained at Wheeler Field. It included players like Ferris Fain, who would later win a couple of batting championships for the Philadelphia Athletics. Tex Hughson, whom I had also faced in the Service League, was also on that squad.

Throughout the winter, we kept playing ball in tropical Hawaii and entertained the troops stationed on the island until June, 1945.

Then we were told of a coming tour of the Far Eastern islands. All who agreed to go on this tour would be allowed to return home right after the war ended. Needless to say, not one of us turned down this offer.

We arrived in Saipan on July 4, 1945. There we built baseball diamonds and played some ball. And, talking about good old country hardball, that's what you had to call playing on a field composed of coral reef. But I didn't care what the field was made of. If the play called for me to slide, so be it. The games were great for the morale of the troops. They may have wanted me and my team to win, but not as badly as I wanted them and *their* team to win that war.

There's no way I can ever forget what those guys and our other veterans have done for this country. To this day, I always visit the Veterans Hospital in Durham, North Carolina, on Valentine's Day.

As for American servicemen, they got to watch the games from bleachers we had built from bomb crates. Sometimes we had as many as 15,000 at a game.

Finally, Japan surrendered and we were shipped back to the States. The mood was pleasant enough as we sailed home, but the waters were churned by winds that reached as high as 90 miles per hour. What was supposed to be an 11 day trip actually lasted 19 days. It was such a rough trip that we weren't allowed to go up on deck for awhile.

Unfortunately, there was also rough sailing ahead in my personal life. Josephine and I had been married in 1943. At first we had lived in Chicago, and then she had moved with me to San Antonio after I joined the service. She stayed with me at the San Antonio Air Base and Cadet Center for two years. When I went overseas she had gone back home to Chicago.

8

I'm ready and rarin' to go," I told the group of sportswriters that had gathered outside St. John's Hospital in St. Louis on February 16, 1946. I'd just been discharged from there after undergoing a minor operation, but the newspapers of that time were reluctant to report the exact nature of my surgery. Things sure had changed by October of 1980. That's when George Brett's hemorrhoids were the number one topic of conversation in the country.

On the first of that month, I had received a more important discharge as far as my baseball career was concerned. That's when I was discharged from the Air Force in San Antonio.

I re-entered major league baseball the way I left it — with mixed emotions. I was ecstatic that the war was over and that I was able to rejoin my beloved Cardinals, but my new divorce from Josephine weighed on my mind pretty heavily at times.

I was also unhappy that, after the year I had in 1942 and the career I had playing ball in the service, the Cardinals didn't see fit to give me a raise. They told me that I was an old man. I was going to turn 30 on April 23. As it turned out, I only had 16 seasons of playing ball left in me. Anyway, I went ahead and signed for the same $11,000 I'd made in 1942. I just wanted to play ball.

I couldn't wait to join the old ballclub in St. Petersburg. When I finally arrived at the park, it was as if I were stepping onto my very own "Field of Dreams." The grass at Al Lang Field never looked greener than when I first set foot on it that spring. Of course, any grass would have looked green compared to those coral reefs during my Far Eastern tour with the servicemen. What a great feeling it was to be able to put on that Cardinal uniform again! How wonderful it was to see Terry, Stan, and all my old teammates as well as the new ones I had been reading about during the past three seasons.

Someone else I enjoyed meeting that spring was a young lady by the name of Mary Peterson Walker. Her husband had been killed in the service, and she had a two-year-old son named Rex who never had a chance to get to know his father. She had a job in Galesburg, but just happened to be down in St. Petersburg for a beach vacation when the Cardinals were training that spring. That's how I got to know her.

The returning Cardinals, who had finished second in 1945 after winning two pennants while I was away, were considered near-invincible by the baseball world when they were joined by the 14 of us coming back from the war. Sportswriters liked to write that Breadon had a better team coming back from the service than he did returning from the previous National League season.

Not all the guys from the '42 club were back. All the talent on the post-war roster gave Breadon a chance to sell some players and increase his bank account. In January, he got $30,000 from the Pirates for Jimmy Brown. Brown was 35 at the time and had only one more season of big league ball left in him.

The same day he sold Brown to Pittsburgh, Breadon peddled Walker Cooper to the Giants for $165,000. So what if he was the best catcher in baseball, Sam reasoned. He figured that veteran Ken O'Dea could do the job, especially when the team had a defensive whiz named Del Rice to back him up. Furthermore, there were a couple of promising backstops coming up from the farm system. I felt that Del Wilber, who had been my manager in the Air Force league, was ready to be a catcher in the major leagues. Also, a personable youngster from St. Louis named Joe Garagiola had been receiving raves from the scouts.

As far as I'm concerned, letting Walker go was the biggest mistake Breadon ever made. He may have parted with bigger names like Dean, Medwick, and Mize, but he was still able to develop a team that won four pennants in five years. I honestly believe that, with that tough, raw-boned catcher behind the plate for us instead of for the Giants, we could have remained a dynasty for another five or six years.

Mort Cooper was gone also. Both of the Coopers had skipped the city series with the Browns the previous spring. They had led the Cardinals to a World Series victory over their crosstown rivals, then were told by Breadon that they couldn't get a raise because all player salaries were frozen because of the war. Then, after both had signed reluctantly for the same money they had made in 1944, they found out that Marty Marion had successfully held out for a raise. Marion was coming off a season in which he had been voted the National League's MVP; nevertheless, the Coopers felt they had been hoodwinked. Walker joined the Navy early in the season, after playing in only four games. But it was Mort who kept going AWOL. He didn't make it to the train station once when the Cardinals headed for Cincinnati. On a day Southworth had him scheduled to pitch against the Bees, Mort went to the Boston Airport instead of the ballpark and flew back to St. Louis. After that stunt, Breadon dealt his former MVP to the team he wouldn't pitch against. In exchange, the Bees sent $60,000 and a red-headed relief pitcher named Charles Barrett.

There's another example of Breadon's luck. Before that trade, Red Barrett was better known for winning jitterbug contests than winning ballgames. But after joining the Cardinals, he went 21-9 and led the National League in victories, innings, and complete games. For Mort, it was all downhill from there.

Mort Cooper going to Boston was one thing, but Billy Southworth's departure to the same club was really a shock. The Braves offered him a lot more money than Breadon would have paid a manager, and after the 1945 world Series, Southworth decided to take him up on the deal.

That was bad news to me, but there was also good news. After releasing Southworth from the last year of his contract, Breadon flew down to Texas to call on another former minor league manager of mine. Eddie Dyer, who had helped turn my career around in 1936 when I was playing for him at Columbus, Georgia, had left the Cardinals organization after the 1944 season to go into the oil business in Houston. Eddie was actually quite satisfied with his life as an entrepreneur, but his associates offered to run the company and his wife talked him into accepting when Breadon offered him Southworth's old job.

"With Eddie Dyer's knowledge of young players, gained through years of experience in our organization, there isn't another man in the country so fitted to run our postwar Cardinals," crowed Breadon, adding, "I think I am the luckiest man in the world."

I thought he was, too. And I was happy to have Dyer as my manager. Billy had been like a father to me, but Eddie was like a brother.

After Lou Klein jumped to the Mexican League, Red Schoendienst became our regular second baseman. In the minor leagues, Red was a shortstop. As a Cardinal rookie in 1945, Schoendienst had been the team's leftfielder. With Musial, Moore and me back, he became an infielder again, but the shortstop job belonged to Marty Marion.

Red was a great second baseman. Seven times he led the league in fielding average at that position. He was a really unselfish player. He'd be willing to help out at short, third or the outfield, if that's where the manager thought he was needed most. And he did a good job for us wherever he played.

Not only was he a top-notch defensive player, but also one of the best switch hitters in the game. He wasn't known for his power, but he could hit them out on occasion. He was an excellent lead-off hitter who could get the extra base.

When I arrived in St. Petersburg, my hemorrhoid problem was gone. Eddie Dyer never had to ask me if I was tired. I hustled every moment I was on the ballfield. I was the first major league ballplayer to score a run in a spring training contest. And, as it turned out, I was to be the last player to score a run in the World Series that year.

The Cardinals were overwhelming favorites to win the pennant. Out of 150 writers in an A.P. poll that spring, only four predicted another team to win the N.L. flag. Our new manager was said to be understating the situation when he said, "If we are no worse than five games behind on the Fourth of July, we should win."

Pittsburgh did beat us Opening Day, but then we showed the world what we were made of and won our next seven straight. Throughout the month of May, we ran neck and neck with the Dodgers. Brooklyn also had a lot of boys coming back from the war and were surprising everybody except themselves. At least, that's what they were saying.

One guy the Dodgers could never beat that year was Max Lanier. The North Carolina southpaw really had a whammy on Brooklyn. The first four times he faced those guys that year, he beat them. In fact, he beat everybody. Lanier pitched six games for us that season. He started, finished and won six, while giving up less than two runs a game. It seemed as though the man could do nothing wrong.

Then Max Lanier made what I feel was a big mistake. He jumped to the Mexican League. So did second baseman Lou Klein, and for that matter, righthanded pitcher Fred Martin.

I didn't know Klein that well. He was a New Orleans boy who had become a valuable second baseman for the Cardinals in 1943, my first year in the Air Force. He also helped out at shortstop that year while playing every inning of every game in the Red Birds second straight pennant-winning season. Shortly thereafter, he went into the service and didn't make it back until late in the 1945 season. In '46, Klein wasn't used as much as during his rookie season, but Dyer liked him. Red Schoendienst was a better hitter, but Dyer still used Klein in certain situations over Red.

Martin was a rookie that year, even though he was 10 months older than I. This was due, at least partially, to the fact that he was one of the first professional ballplayers to join the armed forces during World War II and one of the last to be discharged. He then, in my opinion, marred his fine patriotic record by quitting his ballclub and leaving the United States. Here this man was finally, after all the years in the minor leagues and in the service, getting his chance to play in the big leagues. What did he do with it? He threw it away!

The Mexican League was the closest thing to the sort of free agency that exists in major league baseball today. It had started about the time I reached the Cardinals, but the operators didn't really try to attract big leaguers at first. When World War II ended, things started to change. There were a lot of disgruntled guys like Lou Klein, who were unable to reclaim their regular status when they returned. And the starters who wound up being bumped by returning servicemen were even more upset.

Any such conflict in the case of my reclaiming the Cardinals right field job was settled four days after my discharge from the service. After I had joined the Air Force, my replacement was none other than Stan Musial, who had been shifted by Southworth from left to right field. By 1945, however, Musial had also entered the service and Johnny Hopp was the rightfielder. On February 5, the same day Breadon dealt away Walker Cooper and Jimmy Brown, he peddled Hopp to Boston, where he could continue to play for Southworth. The exchange was for Eddie Joost, a veteran infielder whose primary distinction may have been batting .185 in 1943, the lowest single season average in history for any major league ballplayer with at least 400 at-bats. Of course, the Braves also sweetened that deal, to the tune of about forty grand.

Joost quit the game. He knew he couldn't make any money playing for Sam Breadon when he had to compete for playing time in an infield with the likes of Marty Marion, Red Schoendienst, Whitey Kurowski, and Lou Klein. And Klein knew he couldn't make much money now that Schoendienst was being moved back to second base.

For that matter, Fred Martin probably wanted to see some money for all those years he had toiled in the minor leagues, and Max Lanier felt that he deserved big bucks for his accomplishments.

This, then, was the chance for Jorge Pasquale, who operated the Mexican League, to make his move. With many ballplayers hacked off about the money situation and the sudden overflow of competition, he raided 23 regular players from major league teams. Lanier, Klein, and Martin jumped the club on May 23 that year. I understand that Lanier got $75,000, or at least promises for that amount, from Pasquale. Now, that was a lot of money, but I think he ended up hurting himself in the long run.

There were others. And there could have been more. There weren't too many stars who weren't approached by at least one of the Pasquale brothers. I know Ted Williams was. Musial, Moore, and I were approached by Jorge Pasquale not too long after the others had left the club. We all turned him down. Pasquale contacted me about the same time he made offers to Terry and Stan. I don't know about the other two St. Louis outfielders, but I didn't get any figure from him. He probably knew that I wasn't going to seriously consider leaving the Cardinals after I had dreamed of rejoining them for so long.

For our loyalty, all three of us were given a raise by Breadon. In my case, it was $2,500, for a total salary of $13,500. For that I was grateful, even though I had been disappointed not to get a raise when I first came back. Also, I was starting to worry about the World Series money I had been counting on since spring training.

The Dodgers were also affected by this mess. Mickey Owen, their number one catcher since we had sold him to Brooklyn before the war, jumped to Mexico in pursuit of more dollars. So did Luis Olmo, a 26-year-old Puerto Rican who had become the Dodgers left fielder during the war, and who in 1945 led the league with 13 triples.

Despite the loss of this pair, the Dodgers started to pull away from us. After the May 23 announcement of the defections of Lanier, Klein and Martin, we dropped three of our next four games. Meanwhile, the Dodgers kept pulling away.

I was disappointed in the Mexican Leaguers who I thought were going to be around to help us win the pennant, but we had other problems, too. None of the Cardinals had to give up their life to the Allied cause, like Billy Southworth, Jr., but, as players, we still lost some promising guys to the war. John Grodzicki, a strapping, highly-regarded mound prospect before the war, had his thighs drilled with German bullets. When he tried to pitch again, he found that he could no longer make the pivot. The righthander from Nanticoke, Pennsylvania, never won another game in the majors.

Another immeasurable loss of talent struck the Cardinals when Johnny Beazley developed arm problems when he pitched Air Force ball. I had heard that he failed to warm up properly before a game, but whatever the reason, he lost some of what he had in 1942.

Some of our guys suffered from other injuries. Catcher Ken O'Dea, who was expected to take the place of Walker Cooper, went down with a bad spine and was eventually sold to the Braves. In May, Emil Verban was traded to the Braves for Clyde Klutz, a stocky part-time catcher.

Dyer ended up counting mostly on Del Rice and Joe Garagiola to help us behind the plate. Del was a terrific receiver who could handle pitchers and throw out baserunners, but he couldn't hit a lick and he ran like he had a piano on his back. Joe, a local boy from the Italian area of St. Louis known as The Hill, was only 20 years old and had spent the previous two years in the service.

In place of Sanders, who had been sold to the Braves, the Cardinals were counting on another returning war veteran, Dick Sisler, though he had no major league experience. But he had looked good in Navy ball and really promising in the Cuban Winter League. By now, Dick was 25 years old, and the Cardinals thought he was ripe to display some resemblance to his famous father. Always looking for an extra buck, Breadon figured that by playing Dick, he could attract some old fans of George Sisler, who was, at that time, the greatest player in St. Louis history. Playing for the Browns, first baseman George twice hit over .400 and was one of the first players to make the Hall of Fame. As it turned out, our first baseman that year became an even greater player, in most people's opinion, than George. But it wasn't going to be Dick. The younger Sisler proved to be nothing like his Dad, and Dyer replaced him by bringing Stan in from left field to hold down first.

With Stan at first, left field was a weak spot for us that year. Harry Walker started off out there, but couldn't seem to hit like he did before he had joined the service. We were having problems in centerfield, too. Terry's legs were starting to give out on him. Dyer ended up using Harry Walker a lot in center that year.

Durocher kept telling the reporters that the Dodgers weren't even concerned about the Cardinals. "The Cubs are the team we've got to beat," he kept saying.

Eddie Dyer was hopping mad at Leo's comments and used them to fire up his team. "We'll show The Lip the team he has to beat," he told anyone who wanted to listen. But, in late June, the Dodgers started a win streak which stretched to seven games by July 2. We had just lost four in a row and were at our lowest point of the season, seven and one-half games out.

Then, we started to pick up the pace a bit. We'd knocked three games off that lead by July 12, when they arrived in St. Louis for a four game series. The battle with our first place foes started with a doubleheader victory over our unhappy guests. The second game lasted until the 12th inning when Musial ended it with a home run.

We made it three in a row the next day, and in the fourth game, we went into the bottom of the ninth behind 4-2. Then, with two men on, Dyer brought in a utility player from Chicago named Erv Dusak to pinch hit; Erv responded to the occasion by sending the ball over the fence. To this day, the man is still known as "Four Sack" Dusak because of that home run.

That four game sweep over the Dodgers put us only a half game out of first. It also brought Howie Pollet his 10th victory of the season. Pollet was turning out to be a godsend for us, especially after Lanier and Martin had left for the Mexican League. Not only was he pitching well, but he was pitching a lot. Pollet and Dyer were no strangers. In 1938 Eddie had gone to the lefthander's hometown of New Orleans to watch him pitch in American Legion ball. He signed him and by the following season, he was managing his new prospect at Houston.

That first year, Howie, not even 18, wasn't quite ready for the Buffaloes, as the Houston club was called in those days. The Cardinals sent him down to New Iberia, but both of the following two years he won 20 games for Dyer at Houston. A mutual admiration developed between the two. Eddie hired his pitcher to work at his insurance company in Houston during the off-season. When Howie went off to war, he appointed Eddie as his power-of-attorney.

After the Mexican defections, Pollet had approached his minor league manager, off-season boss, power-of-attorney, and present manager. He told him that he could start every four days and also a game in relief between his starts. Eddie had taken his pal up on that offer and Howie was the workhorse of the National League that year.

Pollet was a pleasant surprise on a pitching staff full of disappointments. In addition to Beazley's and Grodzicki's war-related injuries, Red Barrett could muster up only three victories against the post-war competition of 1946 after winning 23 for the Cardinals the year before.

A couple of days after we swept the Dodgers, we took over first place, but on July 24, Brooklyn went back into first. They stayed on top for the next month. It seemed like we could do well against them, even without our "Dodger killer" Max Lanier, but we seemed to have trouble against the also-rans in the league.

Despite our problems, the hitting of Stan and myself and the pitching of Howie kept us close enough to the top to show Durocher which team he had to beat. When the Bums arrived at Sportsmans Park to begin a four game series on August 25, we were dead even. They beat Pollet 3-2 that day, the durable southpaw's first setback in three weeks. But before the day was done, we were back in a tie with our arch rivals after beating them 14-8 in the second game of a doubleheader.

The next day, Murry Dickson, another guy who wasn't afraid to put in some innings, beat them 4-1 and we were back in the lead. Higbe beat us 7-3 the next day, tying us up once again.

It was really a dogfight the rest of the way. The rivalry had escalated higher than ever. Durocher may have had his team fired up, but he had us fired up, too. Two-and-a-half games was as big a lead as either team would have for the rest of the season. During the next two weeks, Durocher's boys won nine out of ten, but they were still a game and a half behind us when we arrived in Ebbets Field on September 12. We cooled them off as soon as the bell rang by scoring five runs in the first inning. Pollet was in fine form, holding the mighty Dodgers to five hits in that contest.

The 10-2 victory to open the series felt great, but it was can-celed the next day when the Dodgers got to George Munger. Al-most 33,000 fans came to Ebbets Field to watch the third game. That pushed the Dodgers season attendance over the 1.5 million mark, breaking the all-time attendance record set by the Cubs in 1929. Ballclub owners were starting to make money like they never had before, and players, especially those in the big cities, were starting to see larger paychecks. (Too bad I was "over the hill" at age 30.) Well, the Brooklyn fans left the ballpark happy, as Ralph Branca, a seldom-used young righthander, shut us out, leaving them nipping at our heels.

With that slim half-game lead, we started a doubleheader against the Giants with a 3-0 shutout by Murry Dickson. We won the second game, too, but in the process, we may have wound up losing more than we did when those three guys jumped to Mexico. Al Brazle, a sharp-dressing lefthander back from the war after an impressive debut in 1943, had a 5-1 lead in the eighth when the Giants' powerful lineup started to get to him. Outfielder Sid Gor-don was at bat with men on second and third and one run in. Dyer turned to the recently returned Red Munger to put out the fire, but Gordon lined the riqhthander's pitch into left field for a base hit, scoring two. With lefthanded-hitting Babe Young stepping to the plate as the potential winning run, Dyer called for his trusted southpaw, Howie Pollet.

Unbeknownst to Dyer, Howie hadn't even warmed up. He took his eight warmup pitches on the mound before firing the first pitch to Young. Young eventually drove in a run with an infield single. That put the Giants just one run down, but Pollet shut them out for the rest of the game. The actual damage began on that first pitch to Young when Howie felt a burst of pain explode in his shoulder.

No one realized it at the time, but young Howie Pollet would never be the same pitcher again. Not only did he finish that game with what now would be officially listed as a save, but he went nine innings two days later and beat the Giants 10-2 for his 20th win of the year, Who cared if he gave up 11 hits? We had given him plenty of runs to work with. But, as it turned out, for the rest of the season, he had to pamper his left arm.

The Dodgers were hit with a more obvious injury problem on September 26, when Pete Reiser, whose 34 stolen bases were by far the major league high that year, broke his leg as he was sliding back into first base in a game against the Phillies. Even without their speedy left fielder, the Bums caught up with us after being on our heels for over a month. They tied us on September 28 when Howie was pounded by the Cubs for the second time in a row.

The next day, the Dodgers took the lead in the afternoon by defeating Boston. But Harry Brecheen, a wiry southpaw from Broken Bow, Oklahoma, held the Cubs to four hits, and we went into the last day of the season tied with our archrivals from Brooklyn.

We lost to the Cubs and Johnny Schmitz that day by the score of 8-3. Fortunately for us, our old hero Mort Cooper did us a big favor by shutting out the Dodgers. For the first time in baseball history, two clubs had tied at the end of the regular season.

Major league baseball prepared for its first playoff. The National League by laws called for a best-of-three series to determine the pennant winner. The World Series had to be postponed. Joe Cronin, manager of the Boston Red Sox, whose team had clinched the American League flag, was hopping mad. There never had been a dead heat in his league, but such a tie would have been settled in a one-game playoff. The former shortstop hollered that our league didn't need a three-game playoff if his league required only one.

As National League president Ford Frick flipped a coin, Breadon called for heads and it landed tails. Durocher chose for the opener to be played in St. Louis so that the series would then move to Ebbets Field.

Scalpers were asking for as much as ten dollars for regular tickets (which they had paid $1.75 for) and twenty dollars for box seats for the historic meeting at Sportsmans Park. There wasn't that kind of money to go around back then, and the scalpers were caught holding too many tickets. Just before the game, they were trying to unload their tickets for a dollar each, but many folks who had wanted to watch the game must have been by a radio instead of milling around the park. The Cardinals wound up drawing barely over 26,000. They had drawn 8,000 more for that Cubs game two days before.

The ailing Pollet went up against the young Branca. Ralph didn't fool us this time. We got as many hits off him in the first inning as we had the whole game when we had last faced him, and won 4-2.

After a day of travel, we played Game 2 in Brooklyn. The Dodgers drew first blood, but from the second inning until the ninth, Brooklyn fans were forced to watch their chances for a third game grow slimmer. Dusak became, for one precious moment, "Three-Sack" by hitting a triple and then tying the game on Marty Marion's sacrifice fly. Murry Dickson, a good-hitting pitcher who had batted .277 for us that season, tripled off Hatten to put us ahead the same inning.

In the fifth, Hatten had two out when he gave up a double to Musial. Durocher had his southpaw walk righthanded-hitting Whitey Kurowski so that he could pitch to me. That didn't bother me. I always felt that I hit lefthanders as well as I did righthanders. I lined a shot between Furillo and Dixie Walker, tripling in both baserunners. When Dusak batted me in with a single, we were ahead 5-1 and Hatten was through for the season.

Durocher kept bringing new guys to the mound, but that couldn't keep us from padding the lead. In the seventh, Marion batted another run across, this time with a squeeze bunt. In the eighth, Red Schoendienst got a base hit, Terry Moore hit a ground rule double, and Kurowski knocked them in with a single to right.

And Murry's pitching was even better than his hitting that all-important day. At least it was for most of the game. After first baseman Ed Stevens drove in third baseman Augie Galan with a base hit up the middle, the durable pitcher held the Dodgers hitless until the ninth.

The Dodger bats finally came alive as their backs were against the wall in the bottom of the ninth. Galan doubled and Stevens tripled him in. Furillo singled and took second on a wild pitch. After ball four to Pee Wee Reese, Dyer replaced Dickson with

Harry Brecheen. Harry was scheduled to pitch the next day if we lost, but with a five run lead, Dyer wanted to end it right there.

Brecheen wasn't able to put out the fire right away. Catcher Bruce Edwards knocked in Furillo to make the score 8-4, and Cookie Lavagetto drew a walk. Harry finally put an end to the National League season by striking out Eddie Stanky and, for the final out, Barney Schultz.

Brooklyn fans stormed onto the field as we players tried our damndest to get off. Since Dyer had approached me about hustling in the minors, I had always exited the field from my position in right as fast as possible. This time, I had other reasons to get out of there. The Dodgers hadn't given these fans a pennant, so the looters on the field were grabbing for anything they could get their hands on. Someone got my cap, but that was all right by me. I was just glad to be in a World Series again.

Most of the experts favored Boston to wind up as the champions. The Red Sox had never lost a World Series, and their superstar Ted Williams was expected to play better than ever now that he had finally made it to his first one. Both second baseman Bobby Doerr and shortstop Johnny Pesky were threats with the bat and saviors with the glove. For good measure, owner Tom Yawkey had acquired first baseman Rudy York, one of the league's most respected power hitters, from the Detroit Tigers at the beginning of the year. The Red Sox pitching staff, led by 25-game winner Boo Ferris and 20-game winner Tex Hughson, was also intimidating.

The sportswriters and other so-called experts kept saying the Red Sox were the better of the two teams "on paper." That didn't bother me one bit because the 1942 Yankees had also been the best team "on paper." But that didn't give them a world championship.

"The Red Sox have got to show us," I kept telling the reporters and, for that matter, anyone who wanted to listen. "They've got to beat us on the field."

On October 6, we hosted the opener at Sportsmans Park. It was a duel between Tex Hughson and our Howie Pollet. Hughson, a tall, durable righthander, could really fire a fastball, and also had a mean curve. He had been as good as any pitcher in the American

League since 1942. That day, I got a triple off him, but it didn't account for any scoring. Hughson left the game in the top of the ninth for pinch-hitter Jack Partee. Cronin brought in a lefthander named Earl Johnson, a lanky Swede from Washington state. He reminded me of Stan Hack the way he kept smiling on the mound. He held us scoreless in the ninth. We headed for extra innings knotted up at 2-2.

Rudy York, the powerful part-Cherokee who had banged 249 homers in his 10 years with the Tigers, added another round-tripper onto the top of the left field stands. It was probably the only bad pitch Pollet had thrown the whole game, but it was enough for our ace to lose that day. In the bottom of the 10th, Johnson, a decorated war hero from the Battle of the Bulge, became a World Series hero by holding us scoreless once again and winning the first game for Boston.

In game number two, Brecheen was given his long-awaited chance to start while the Red Sox sent up a boy from New York City named Mickey Harris. Harris wasn't the best pitcher Cronin had available to start, but he was the best lefthander. With a 17-9 record, the southpaw, who had spent the previous four years in the army, had enjoyed his finest major league season. The Red Sox manager was quite aware that we Cardinals had been suffering our share of trouble against lefties, and figured that we'd have our problems against Harris.

Cronin turned out to be right on that count. As a team, we didn't hit that well against Harris. I didn't hit him at all. Neither did Musial nor Schoendienst. But our own lefthander was better. Harry shut them out on four hits. We got all the scoring we needed from the bottom of the order. In the third, Del Rice got hold of a pitch and drove it against the left field wall. As slow as he was, our backup catcher scored when Brecheen followed with a single to right. For good measure, Del also started a two-run rally with a base hit to left in the fifth, and we tied the Series with a 3-0 victory.

Two days later, after the Series had shifted to Boston, Cronin finally sent his ace against us. Ferris had seen his Air Force career cut short because of asthma, but that didn't stop him from throw-

ing a baseball. As a major league rookie, Boo had won 21 games
for the Bosox in 1945. The following year, with more returning
veterans like Ted Williams on his team, the righthander from Mississippi was even better, going 25-6.

Dyer countered with Murry Dickson. Murry surely deserved
the start, but unfortunately for us, he got off to a rocky one. In the
first inning Rudy York hurt us again. With two men on, York
worked a full count against Dickson and then hammered a pitch
against the screen on top of the left field wall.

Ferris showed us that day why he was the best pitcher on the
American League's best team by holding us to six hits. No man
reached third until Musial in the ninth, with two outs. We were
blanked 4-0, and the Sox led two games to one.

I was disappointed, but not discouraged. There was now talk
of the Red Sox taking the next two and finishing us off there in
Boston. I said that there was no way the series wasn't going back
to St. Louis.

I meant what I said, and proved it the next day with a home
run in the second inning off Hughson, to add to a double and two
singles. It felt good going four-for-six after having to settle for
only two hits in my first 12 World Series at-bats that year. In all,
we got 20 hits that game, embarrassing the Red Sox 12-3.

The final game at Fenway, once again, gave the Boston fans
something to holler about. It also pushed our backs against the
wall. After 266 innings during the regular season and ten tough
innings during the Series opener, Pollet just didn't have it. He gave
up three hits and had only one out in the first when Dyer replaced
him with Alpha Brazle.

Righthander Joe Dobson took to the mound for the Red Sox
in that game. Twenty years before in Durrant, Texas, the young
lad was playing with a firecracker and blew off his left thumb and
index finger. His right arm was really firing those baseballs,
though. He struck out eight Cardinals. He also struck me in the
right elbow with a fastball in the fifth inning.

Damn right, it hurt, but I wasn't about to rub it and give Dobson the pleasure of seeing me in pain. Instead, I tossed the bat
away with my right hand, hustled down to first base and promptly

stole second. Nobody drove me in, and as I patrolled right field in the bottom of the inning, I could feel my arm swelling. By the time I was supposed to go up to the plate again, the flesh around my elbow was so bloated that I couldn't even swing a bat. It hurt as bad as my elbow did to go up to Eddie and tell him, but I knew I would only be dragging the Cardinals down if I tried to stay in the game.

"I can't do you any good. You'd better take me out," I told Dyer, with the saddest expression I ever had on my face in a baseball dugout. I had never asked to leave a ballgame before, and here I was doing it right in the middle of a World Series.

Trainer Doc Weaver and I headed to the clubhouse where he turned on the radio and put ice packs around my arm. Still, the painful throbbing persisted. Listening to the Red Sox nail down the 6-3 victory to put them one game away from the championship didn't help our spirits, either.

At least we were going back to St. Louis to finish the Series, despite the predictions of some of the Eastern sportswriters. Yawkey flew his club west so that his guys could get an extra day's rest. The Cardinals took a sleeper, but I couldn't sleep at all that night on the train with my elbow in such pain. Doc had me in one of those electric jackets relief pitchers wore in those days. It may have helped those guys on cold days in the bullpen, but it didn't do me much good.

At first, things didn't get any better after our train arrived in St. Louis. I went straight from the train station back to St. John's Hospital where I was met by Dr. Hyland.

He immediately X-rayed my swollen elbow. According to the Cardinals' physician, my problems went beyond discomfort.

"I sure hate to tell you this, but you just can't play in the Series any more," he said in a somber tone.

"I'm playing," I replied.

"The hemorrhaging around your elbow is really bad," the doctor continued. "If it were to be hit against the ground, with another ball or against the fence, you'd be through as a player. I mean it. In fact, I'd have to amputate your arm."

"I'm just going to have to take that chance," I said. "If I can swing a bat, I'll be out there."

The next day, there was still pain and swelling around my elbow, but I could swing a bat. At my insistence, Dyer put me into the lineup.

Game Six was a rematch between southpaws Mickey Harris and Harry Brecheen. In the first inning, Harris continued his hold on me and struck me out. After two innings the game was a scoreless tie.

In the bottom of the third, we got to Harris. Rice started it off for us with a single, but was forced at second on Brecheen's grounder. Then Schoendienst lashed a curveball for a double, and Brecheen scored on Moore's sacrifice fly. Then it was single, single, single. Musial moved Schoendienst to third, Kurowski knocked him in, and I drove home Stan.

Brecheen continued his dominance over the Red Sox, much to the chagrin of Mickey Harris, who swore that he had better stuff. "My changeup is faster than Brecheen's fastball," the New Yorker moaned to reporters after the game.

As it turned out, Harry didn't need his fastball; his screwball did the trick. After shutting out the Sox for 15 consecutive innings, our crafty southpaw was finally touched for a run in the bottom of the seventh when York tripled and scored on a sacrifice fly.

Back in the clubhouse after our 4-1 victory, my spirits were soaring. My elbow still hurt, but I could still swing a bat. More importantly, we had caught the Sox, and I was in a room with some happy guys. Instead of the radio, Doc Weaver had the old Victrola of his blaring out with the 78 record of "Woodchoppers Ball."

"Why don't you guys go over and take a picture of Ted Williams," hollered a jubilant Johnny Beazley to the photographers as they were asking us to pose for them. "He got a hit today."

That's right, Ted Williams got a hit. One harmless single in four trips to the plate. We were handcuffing him that series. From the beginning, Dyer was determined not to let the Splendid Splinter beat us. Dyer set up the defense in a very unorthodox manner against the feared slugger. Whenever Williams would come to the plate, Kurowski would move from third base to the other side of second. Marion would hold his ground at shortstop, but the rest of the fielders would shift considerably to the right. Lou Boudreau, manager of the Cleveland Indians, had also deployed a defense based on the mighty slugger's tendency to pull. It became known as the "Boudreau Shift." Sportswriters started referring to the placement of the Cardinals fielders against Williams as the "Do or Dyer Shift." No matter what people called it, it worked. Years later, I told Ted that if he hadn't been so darn hardheaded and continued to pull the ball when that shift was used on him, he could have hit .400 any time he wanted to. But he just didn't hit in that Series, the only one he would ever have a chance to play in.

"The Red Sox have some fine hitters on their ballclub if you pitch them what they want, but I just didn't do it," yelled the triumphant Brecheen over the cheering and the music.

Granted, Boston had never lost a World Series, not even the Boston Braves, but past history no longer favored them to win the '46 Series. You see, at that point, the Cardinals, who had gone the distance three times before, had never lost the seventh game of a World Series. And this series was going seven games.

"It's our turn to win Tuesday," claimed Tex Hughson in the visitor's clubhouse at Sportsmans Park. "This has been a series of one-game winning streaks. Our turn is coming up."

The oddsmakers sided with Hughson. The Sox were favored 10-7 to win the final game.

Monday was an off day as tickets were sold for the seventh game. On October 15, the two teams met at Sportsmans Park once again to decide once and for all who would be champion. Before the game Dyer received a letter calling us "gangsters" for holding back Ted Williams. Murry Dickson, whom Dyer was counting on to hold back Williams and the rest of the Red Sox just one more time, was making sure he didn't get cheated out of his warmups once again. Ushers checked for cameras in the dugouts and the area of the ballpark where Dickson was throwing so that the blinding flashbulbs wouldn't mess him up like he claimed they had earlier in the Series.

Dickson's start wasn't perfect, but it could have been worse. Wally Moses and Johnny Pesky greeted our hurler with singles and Dom DiMaggio sent Moses home with a sacrifice fly. But that was all the Sox scored until the eighth inning.

Meanwhile, we tied it in our half of the second when Whitey Kurowski tagged Boo Ferris with a two-out double. Then in the fifth, Harry Walker got a base hit off Ferris and scored when Dickson doubled to left to put us ahead. Schoendienst followed with a shot over shortstop Johnny Pesky's outstretched glove, driving in Murry and giving us an insurance run.

After Terry Moore lined a single to center, Ferris was pulled for Joe Dobson. The lanky righthander who had beaten us in the fifth game took care of Musial. Then it was time for me to face Dobson for the first time since he put my career in jeopardy by plunking my right elbow. This time, he gave me a free pass again, but with four balls instead of a fastball against my body. He then retired Kurowski with the bases loaded to stop the bleeding.

Dickson and Dobson each held the opposition scoreless in the sixth and seventh innings. Then they both left the ballgame in the top of the eighth. Dickson had retired 18 of the last 19 Red Sox when Rip Russell, pinch-hitting for catcher Hal Wagner, opened the inning with a base hit. Then Dobson went out for pinch-hitter George "Catfish" Metkovich, a lefthanded outfielder who had been nicknamed by Casey Stengel. Supposedly the nickname came from a freak injury George suffered while removing a fish from a hook. Metkovich didn't look like a catfish. Actually, he looked a little like Ted Williams. Catfish sure as hell didn't hit like Williams, but he outhit the better-known Red Sox outfielder that day when he tagged Dickson for a double along the left field line.

That was it for Dickson. Dyer brought in Brecheen, who had given the Sox fits so far. At first, it looked like Harry's craftiness would get us out of the inning. With runners on second and third and an 0-2 count on Wally Moses, Brecheen snuck a screwball over the plate for a called strike. Next, Pesky batted a harmless fly ball to me, that was too shallow to drive in Russell. Then Dom DiMaggio nailed a screwball that flew over my head. I ran. I leaped. But I still was unable to snare DiMaggio's screaming line drive. By the time I was able to retrieve it, the ball had bounced off the screen in right-center.

When the dust had cleared, DiMaggio was on second base and our lead was gone. But school was out in 1946 for "The Little Professor." DiMaggio was forced to leave the ballgame because he had pulled a muscle in his leg as he rounded first on that game-tying double. Leon Culberson, a Red Sox utility outfielder from Rome, Georgia was brought into the game to run for Dom. This turned out to be an important factor in the final outcome.

Next up, for his final World Series at-bat, was Ted Williams. With the tying run at second, first base open and baseball's mightiest slugger at the plate, you'd think that Eddie Dyer would have had Brecheen walk Williams. But Harry was having a great Series and Ted had been collared that day. Harry went after his man and Ted popped a ball up which Schoendienst easily grabbed to retire the side.

With Dobson out for a pinch-hitter, the new man on the mound in the bottom of the eighth for Boston was Bob Klinger. Klinger and I were no strangers to each other because of his years in the National League with Pittsburgh. In fact, he was the first pitcher I ever faced in the major leagues back in 1938, when we were both rookies. After six seasons of being used primarily as a starter with the Pirates and two years in the U.S. Navy during World War II, Klinger was being used by Cronin exclusively out of the bullpen. It turns out that if records had been kept for saves that year (they weren't), Klinger would have led the American League with a grand total of nine. At the age of 38 Klinger was, for the first time, on a team that made it to the World Series. And in the eighth inning of the seventh game, the righthander from Missouri made his first pitch in that series. I didn't swing at it, but I eventually tagged the ex-Pirate for a clean single.

Klinger fared better against the next two batters. Whitey Kurowski popped up and Del Rice hit a lazy, shallow fly ball. That brought Harry Walker to the plate. Harry had been hitting the ball well in the Series, but he was primarily a singles hitter. I figured the best chance I had of scoring was if I stole second. So I took off.

I heard the crack of the bat, but with two out, there was no need to worry about tagging up. It looked like a routine single to centerfield. But by the time I rounded second base, I was determined not to make it routine. I made up my mind that I was going to score the go-ahead run on that play.

Two factors helped me make that spur-of-the-moment decision, which may have turned out to be the most important one of my entire baseball career.

Before I explain the first factor, let me say right here that I didn't consider Leon Culberson to be a bad ballplayer. He had batted a respectable .319 that year and had hit a home run for Boston earlier in the Series. But as a glove man, Culberson just wasn't in the class of Dominic DiMaggio. Other than Terry Moore, Dom was probably the best defensive centerfielder in baseball at the time. If Joe D.'s brother had been out there to retrieve Walker's hit, I wouldn't have even considered trying to advance three bases on the play.

I also remembered a conversation I had with Dyer after the Series opener. In that first game, I had thought that I had a good shot at an inside-the-park home run off Hughson. But as I approached third base, there was coach Mike Gonzales with his hands in the air telling me to hold up. As it turns out, I didn't score that inning, we ended up tied with the Red Sox at the end of nine, and we lost it in the tenth. In the gloomy clubhouse following the defeat, I approached Eddie.

"Skipper, I could have scored on that triple I hit if I hadn't been held up," I had told him.

"Next time that you think you can score with two out, go ahead and try for it," Dyer replied. "I'll back you up."

Knowing that Eddie was always as good as his word, I didn't care what signal Coach Gonzales was flashing after Walker hit that ball. In fact, I wasn't even looking. My eyes were riveted on the baseline, and my mind was totally focused on making it to home plate as fast as my legs would carry me.

Today, people still question what was on Johnny Pesky's mind after he caught the relay from Culberson. The shortstop was, of course, facing centerfield as he retrieved the throw. His back was to the plate, and there was no way Pesky could have seen "Enos

Slaughter's Mad Dash for Home," as it is now referred to by baseball historians.

In case you don't know, I made it. By the time Pesky realized I was going for the plate, he didn't have a chance. I kicked up some dust, and a few pebbles too, as I slid into the plate. But with the throw drawing catcher Roy Partee out four or five steps in front of home, I could have made it just as well standing up.

A lot of people have crucified Pesky for his momentary freeze on that play, but I don't go along with them. I blame second baseman Bobby Doerr or third baseman Pinky Higgins. Culberson, as it turned out, fielded the ball cleanly and wasted no time firing it back to the infield. Pesky had to have his back toward me as he took the throw. When I rounded third, someone should have been hollering for him to throw the ball home. Years later, Doerr told me that with all the noise of 36,000 screaming home fans at Sportsmans Park, nobody could hear *anything*.

Anyway, the Series didn't end at that moment. There were still some tense moments left in the 1946 season. We took the one run lead into the ninth inning, and the Red Sox immediately threatened. York started it off with a base hit, and was pinch-run for by a younger, swifter Paul Campbell. Doerr, the leading Red Sox hitter for the Series, lifted his postseason average to .409 with another base hit. Then, Doerr was forced out on an infield grounder by Higgins, leaving Boston with men on first and third with one out.

Partee popped a foul, which Musial grabbed near first base. Then Tom McBride, a Texan who had batted over .300 for the Sox as a part-time outfielder the previous two seasons, was sent up to pinch-hit. McBride had tied up the first game with two out in the ninth, and he was raring to do it again. This time, McBride hit a grounder to Schoendienst at second. As Campbell sped for the plate, the ball momentarily seemed to run up Red's arm. But he got hold of the tricky baseball and flipped it to Marion, who was anxiously standing on second.

Higgins was called out on the force play that afternoon, October 15, at exactly 3:47 P.M. That was a happy moment for the Cardinals, but, I understand, a bad time for pigeons in downtown

St. Louis. Those poor birds must have thought all hell had broken loose when the confetti started flying out office windows and horns blared from automobiles on into the fall midwestern night.

9

The off-season was about as pleasant as I could ask for. The only other time I had closed the season out as part of a championship team, I had to leave the Cardinals for the Army. This time, I didn't have to worry about such a thing.

On top of that, I was enjoying being around Mary more and more. She hardly knew a thing about baseball when I first met her, but she had quickly become a fan. I had taught her to like hunting and fishing as well. She'd never done those things before, but when I took her with me on some of these expeditions, she really had a good time. In fact, she actually turned out to be a pretty good hunter. I remember her shooting her limit when we went pheasant hunting.

I decided (once again) that I had found the woman with whom I wanted to spend the rest of my life. In May, we would marry and I would adopt 3-year-old Rex . In 1948, Mary would present me with a beautiful baby daughter, whom we would name Patricia.

I went back to my off-season plan for conditioning. I'd eat all I wanted to up until Thanksgiving Day. After that feast, I'd stay on my diet for the rest of the winter. I was very careful not to eat too much over the Christmas holidays. And, of course, I'd go hunting every time I had a chance. Tramping through those woods along with my dogs kept my legs in shape. The legs normally go first on an athlete, and I was in no hurry for that to happen to me.

Then I would arrive in St. Petersburg for spring training weighing just a few more pounds than I had at the end of the previous season. And, because my elbow had healed over the winter, I was in better shape in the spring of 1947 than I was at the end of the World Series of 1946.

With a brand new championship ring on my finger and a brand new engagement ring on Mary's finger, I showed up at Al Lang Field with a broad smile on my face to greet my fellow returning champions.

Spring training was a happy time for us in 1947. I can't imagine it not being happy when a team gets together in Florida for the first time after having won the World Series the previous October. Sportswriters and oddsmakers overwhelmingly favored us to win the National League pennant again. We headed into the season with the team pretty well intact from the squad which had beaten the Red Sox.

At the time, more attention was being paid to the activities of the Brooklyn Dodgers. Manager Leo Durocher's 1947 spring training had its similarities with Pete Rose's 1989 season. It was common knowledge that Durocher was under investigation by the Commissioner's office. On April 9, just as the season was about to get under way, Commissioner Happy Chandler suspended Durocher for the year because of "association with known and notorious gamblers."

I'm sure that Leo's suspension has a lot to do with his not being in the Hall of Fame today, but I would like to say this for the man: Leo Durocher was a manager I would have loved to have played for, because of the hell-bent-for-leather type of ballplaying he believed in.

The day after Durocher's suspension, Branch Rickey sent a shock wave of his own throughout the baseball world. Infielder Jackie Robinson was being promoted to Brooklyn from the organization's triple-A farm club at Montreal. For the first time since catcher Fleet Walker's last game for the Toledo Mud Hens in 1884, there would be a black ballplayer in major league baseball.

Some sportswriters predicted problems for Brooklyn's new first baseman. They pointed to the fact that sixty percent of ballplayers were from the South. A lot of the Cardinals were Southerners, but I sure don't remember it being any reason for concern on the Cardinals.

If anything bothered us that spring, it was the arm problems of Johnny Beazley. Eddie Dyer had talked him out of retiring the year before and, after the Series, Beazley seemed determined to return to his 1942 form. But what we saw in the spring of '47 was not the Beazley of '42. Just after the season started, he was peddled to the Boston Braves in a straight cash deal. Some of the writers thought that Billy Southworth had the magic touch to return his former 21-game winner to his days of past glory, but things didn't work out that way. During the following three seasons, the Nashville righthander pitched in only thirteen games for Boston.

In my opinion, Southworth was also affected by the war. His son had paid the ultimate sacrifice. Billy Southworth Jr. went down with the Air Force B-29 he commanded on February 16, 1945, in a freak but tragic accident.

I was sad, too, because I knew Billy and his wife. It certainly was a heartbreaking set of circumstances. By the time his father had become manager of the Cardinals, Billy Jr. was in his fifth year as an outfielder in the team's farm system. I think he had a good chance to make the major leagues, but just before Christmas in 1940, he left baseball to join the Air Force as a cadet pilot.

During the war, he led 25 bombing missions over Europe. His planes caught a lot of bullets during these attacks, but neither Billy nor any of his men suffered a scratch during these dangerous expeditions. Fighting the Nazis, he was in a different world from the one he had grown up in, but young Southworth always had a place for baseball in his heart. He'd wear his old baseball caps as he commanded his flights in the war zone, and it is believed that he is the man who got so many other Americans on bombing crews to wear them. His father used to give him baseballs and gloves from the Cardinals to pass along to his own crew.

"I like to manage my crew like Dad manages his Cardinals," the young major liked to say.

Four years out of baseball had diminished the 27-year-old pilot's chances of making it to the Cardinals as a player, but his father's reputation and his own leadership experience from the war made it appear that Billy Jr. still had a bright future in baseball

My father, Zadok Slaughter, as a young man.

That's me, age 11 or 12. This probably was a
school picture; I didn't get dressed up that often
working around the farm.

As a young player tearing up the American Association for the Columbus, Ohio Red Birds in 1937. (Sporting News)

Terry Moore, Coaker Triplett, myself and roommate Don Padgett in 1941. The averages, left to right: .311, .333, .348, and .333. (Wide World Photos)

A locker room victory scene during the 1942 Series. Clockwise from bottom: Billy Southworth, myself, Stan Musial, Terry Moore, Whitey Kurowski, and Harry Walker. (Sporting News)

I was proud to wear two uniforms during military service in World War II. The one on the right helped entertain and lift the morale of our fighting troops, both in the U.S. and in the Pacific.

Spring training, 1946. Feeling good about our chances for the coming year are, left to right: Johnny Beazley, manager Eddie Dyer, and myself. (Sporting News)

Our 8-4 victory over the Dodgers to win the first playoff series in National League history started an on-field celebration (left photos), but a few Brooklyn fans got into the act (right photos) as we tried to leave the field. (Wide World Photos)

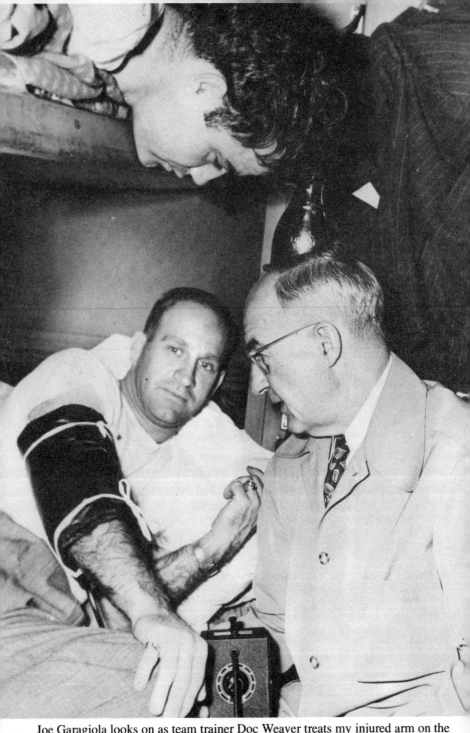

Joe Garagiola looks on as team trainer Doc Weaver treats my injured arm on the train bound for St. Louis and the last two games of the 1946 World Series. (Wide World Photos)

Crossing the plate with the winning run in Game 7 of the 1946 World Series. (Sporting News)

I seldom miss an opportunity to go hunting or
fishing.

My mother, with me in her later years. She
wasn't just a great mom, but a real baseball fan,
too. I took her to a lot of Cardinal games over
the years.

I was really broken up to find out the Cardinals had traded me to the Yankees in early 1954. (Sporting News)

At least the trade sent me to a great club with a great manager. Casey Stengel gave me a warm welcome in Washington, D.C., where the newest Yankee arrived ready, as always, to play ball. (Wide World Photos)

Hank Bauer, left, and Casey Stengel don't seem too worried about my fractured wrist, hurt in a June 1954 tumble while chasing a fly ball. Like most of my other injuries over the years, this one didn't keep me out of the lineup for long. (Wide World Photos)

"Old '41'" still had a few diving catches left in him, like this stab of a line drive off the bat of Jim Lemon during a Yankees-Senators twin bill in 1957. (Wide World Photos)

I enjoyed my years as baseball coach of the Duke Blue
Devils. My family has always rooted for Duke. (Duke
University Sports Information)

Induction day at the Hall of Fame in Cooperstown, 1985. The other guy at
the podium got a few hits during his career, too — Ted Williams. (National
Baseball Library, Cooperstown, N.Y.)

ahead of him. Also, a Hollywood producer had signed the handsome lad to a ten year movie contract.

He was safe from enemy bullets that winter day at La Guardia Airport. The air traffic controllers had given him permission to land, but just as he was ready to hit the ground, they told him to pull up. As he pulled away, the plane veered, crashed into Flushing Bay, and exploded.

I don't think that Southworth ever really recovered from his son's death. I've been told that he started drinking more, and sometimes when the Braves were in New York, he'd go to La Guardia to look for Billy Jr.

The pennant race from the year before renewed the traditional Cardinals-Dodgers rivalry. All through the forties, there had been bad blood between the two clubs. Players on both sides seemed to play their hardest against each other. Ever since Bob Bowman had beaned Joe Medwick in 1940, a free-for-all was likely to break out on the field any time we played in Brooklyn or they played in St. Louis. The fact that our clubs went on to become the top two NL teams of the decade made the competition between us even fiercer. We loved to hate them, and they loved to hate us. By "hate", I don't mean that we wished them any ill will off the ballfield, but we sure as hell weren't about to give any ground while we were between those white lines. The newspaper writers from the respective cities also liked to add fuel to the fire whenever possible. Of course, after our playoff victory over Brooklyn in 1946, the animosity between the two clubs had climbed to new heights.

Robinson not only broke new social ground, he gave the team added offensive punch—more than the Dodgers had from the platooning of Big Bill Stevens and Howard Schultz the year before. Since they had fought us to a regular season tie with those two relatively weak hitters at first base, what would happen if they had a strong hitter at that position? When the season started, our fears turned into reality. The Dodgers took off from opening day, while the Cards couldn't seem to get off the ground. On April 20, a defeat at the hands of the Cubs dropped our defending World

Championship team into last place. Worse yet, that was the beginning of a nine-game losing streak for us.

Ironically, I was off to a good start and among the league leaders in hitting. But Musial was ailing, and as a whole the team wasn't hitting. Our pitchers couldn't seem to get the job done, either. We weren't getting blown away that much during our slump, but when it came down to a crucial pitch in a tight game, our man on the mound always seemed to get tagged for a costly base hit.

In May, things started to turn ugly. There were rumors that this team or that team were divided over the "color line" being broken. The rumors included talk of strikes or other protests. A New York newspaper came out with an article claiming there was talk among the Cardinals of going on strike rather than taking the field at Sportsmans Park against the Dodgers and their new first baseman. That was news to me when I read it in the papers. But it really burned me up to read that I was accused of being a "ringleader" in such a strike movement.

I never even thought about going on strike, much less talked about it. I wanted to play baseball. I always looked forward to playing the Dodgers and, with both teams contending for the pennant, 1947 was certainly no exception. Why in the hell would I have wanted to strike rather than play them? I had spent my entire military career longing for a chance to return to the major leagues. Other than being in another World Series, there was nothing I wanted to do more than play against Brooklyn. Here it was early in the season, we were the defending champions, and Brooklyn was in first place. Hell, yes, I wanted to play against the Dodgers!

There *was* behind-the-scenes talk among the Cardinals —talk of replacing Eddie Dyer. Breadon visited the club with the intention of replacing his manager with one of our fading veteran players. Not me, mind you. In fact, I was off to a good start for a change. But Terry Moore had been slowing down and Marty Marion's back had been acting up on him. Either man was capable of taking over from Dyer, but both passed up the opportunity. Later, Eddie told the writers: "Mr. Breadon talked with Marty

Marion and Terry Moore. One word from them and I would have been out. I'll always remember their loyalty."

Worse for the team than the condition of Moore's legs or Marion's back was the chronic appendicitis that was plaguing Stan Musial. The Man was definitely struggling during the early part of the season. By June his average, which had been in the .350 range the past three seasons, was hovering around the .200 mark. His power numbers, which had been such an important part of the Cardinal attack, were also off. This led to an extremely poor start for our defending championship team.

In an effort to get more home runs, Cardinal management traded outfielder Harry Walker to the Phillies for a stocky out-fielder named Ron Northey. Known as "The Round Man" because of his 5'10", 195-pound frame, Northey was originally inserted by Dyer into left field. While Ron was capable of hitting some balls out for us, his lack of speed was a serious defensive liability. Even though I was regarded as the best rightfielder in the league at the time, I volunteered to switch to left so that Ron could move to right, the position he had played at Philadelphia. It took extra work and practice on my part to get used to my new position, but the shift did prevent some runs against us.

Shortly after the Walker-Northey trade a lesser acquisition was made when Sam Breadon signed a 35-year-old free agent to serve as a pinch-hitter and extra outfielder, Joe Medwick. Since his beaning by Bob Bowman in Brooklyn, Medwick had bounced around the major leagues. He had gone to the Giants, the Braves, the Browns, then back with the Dodgers before moving to the Yankees. The Yankees had released him that spring. Medwick couldn't run anymore, but he was a useful part-time player for us in 1947, his last full year in the big leagues. Joe was a lot nicer guy when he was on his way down than he had been in my early days with the Cardinals.

On June 4, we were deadlocked in a 4-4 tie with the Giants at the Polo Grounds when I led off the 10th inning against the Giants most prominent reliever of the late 1940s, a righthander named Ken Trinkle. I hit a shot over the head of centerfielder Bobby Thompson and took off. Rounding first, second and then third base, I tore for the plate in an effort to score the winning run on an inside-the-park homer. But Walker Cooper was waiting for me at the plate with the ball in his hand. I charged ahead, hoping to jar the ball loose, but it didn't work out that way. I was out at the plate and lost to the club for a week with a sprained ankle.

Adding insult to injury, Ron Northey followed up with a fly ball deep enough to score me if I had held up at third. In the 11th, Willard Marshall homered off Ken Burkhart to beat us. Furthermore, when I did come back, I was not the same. My .358 average declined for the rest of the season, finally dipping below .300.

For the next 50 games I batted at about a .240 clip, but the team was getting better. Two days after my collision with Cooper, the Cardinals made it out of the cellar and Musial's average rose above the .200 mark. By July 11, Stan was above .250 and the team was in fourth. Then The Man went on a tear and raised his average 30 points in two weeks, helping the Cards reach second place in the process. It was a distant second, mind you, but we continued to close the gap. By the time Musial reached .300 in early August, we were only three games out.

I'm not insinuating that Stan got us from last place to contention by himself. The pitching improved quite a bit also. The most dramatic turnaround was by Murry Dickson, who went 9-3 after losing his first seven decisions.

As the race continued into the dog days of August, the Dodgers gained some ground, but we weren't about to let up.

On August 20, Ralph Branca had a no-hitter against us going into the eighth inning. Just over a month before, I had spoiled a no-hit bid by this same Dodger pitcher when I lined his first pitch of the eighth inning to right field for a base hit. But this time Whitey Kurowski opened up the eighth by singling on a 3-2 count.

Still, Branca had a one-hit shutout and a two-run lead going for him in the ninth when he walked Schoendienst and then me. Northey was up next, and Branca's first two pitches to Ron were wide. That was all of Branca Shotton could take that day. The Dodger manager brought in Hugh Casey, but the ace reliever was unable to put out the fire that day. Northey singled in Red and drove me to third. I scored the tying run when third baseman Spider Jorgenson bobbled Kurowski's grounder.

No one scored in the 10th. In the 11th, I was up to bat again. I hit what appeared to be a harmless infield grounder and ran like hell to first. Why shouldn't I? If I hadn't been hustling when Kurowski hit that grounder in the ninth, I wouldn't have tied the score. Robinson was covering first. He had been a middle infielder throughout his early career, but the Dodgers had Eddie Stanky at second base and Pee Wee Reese playing shortstop at the time, so they converted him to first base, where they had the greatest need.

Now, if you are covering second base, it's okay to have your foot square in the middle of the bag, because on a close play the runner has to slide. But, it's a different situation at first. Anyway, the throw to Robinson was low. He had to step forward to scoop up the throw, and when he stepped back on the base for the putout, his foot was right in the middle of the bag. If I were going to slide like you do when you're headed into second base on a close play, nothing would have happened. But this play was at first base, where a runner is allowed to run past, and the object is to get there as fast as you can. I had always played by the rule that the basepaths belong to the runner, and I don't believe I have to apologize for not making an exception to this for anyone. On this occasion, my spikes clipped his ankle.

Robinson wasn't seriously injured. In fact, he didn't even leave the game. I didn't really think a whole lot about it at the time because I knew that Robinson wasn't hurt. When Kurowski homered to end the game in the 12th, I went to the locker room happy.

Soon, though, I was angry. It was the trash that some writers put into their accounts of this so-called "incident" that made my blood boil. They claimed I had spiked Robinson deliberately. They even started attributing the friction between the Cardinals and the Dodgers to Robinson's presence. Hell, the two teams had been fighting like cats and dogs for the entire decade, but now that Jackie had been promoted to Brooklyn, the writers said the two teams fought because the Cardinals were prejudiced.

Now, I'd spiked a lot of guys that I hadn't intended to because they had their foot blocking the basepaths. The color of Robinson's skin was the farthest thing from my mind while I was trying to beat out the low throw to first base. Still, it was claimed that I had cut Robinson because he was black.

The stories kept on coming. In Philadelphia, Musial was unable to play because of his appendicitis. From there, the Cardinals headed to New York and there were headlines saying that Stan and I had gotten in a fight over the Robinson thing, that I had punched Musial in the stomach.

We hadn't said one word to each other about the Robinson incident, but that's the kind of thing some writers put into their stories up there.

Later, we were playing the Giants at the Polo Grounds and I was sliding into second base and spiked Bill Rigney. He needed 23 stitches in his hand. That didn't make headlines. Another time, playing against the Dodgers, we were attempting a double steal, and as second baseman Eddie Stanky was jumping for the ball, I hit him and knocked him into left field. He was carried off on a stretcher, but they don't talk about these things the way they talk about the Robinson play.

People started calling me a dirty player, but I didn't see it that way. I was just trying to win ballgames. Helping the team win was my bread and butter, and I wasn't about to let any player come between it.

I still don't believe any strike plan existed among the players on my team. By then, I was one of the senior members of the team, and such serious talk would have come my way if it actually existed. Maybe someone had made some comments in jest, but I can't imagine anyone on that team not wanting to play ball.

The only games I missed that year were due to injuries. I missed one game after I was hit in the mouth by a ball thrown by Phillies catcher Andy Seminick as I tried to score on a passed ball. I missed five more when I sprained my ankle sliding into home in a game against the Giants. The last game I missed came after I collided into the knee of a reserve shortstop named Bernie Creger as we were both chasing a pop fly. I was out cold for six hours after that one.

These injuries didn't do much for my batting average. With three stitches in my mouth, an ankle bound so tight that I couldn't move my toes, and a pain in my neck that hung on through the following winter, I finished the season at .291. It was the first time I had batted below .300 since my rookie year in 1938. Once again, I scored 100 runs. It was the third consecutive season I had done so.

After the season, Sam Breadon decided that it was time for him to get out of baseball. He sold the club to a group of St. Louis businessmen, including Fred Saigh and Bob Hannegan, who was the Postmaster-General. Some of the players were delighted at the news of the sale because they thought that it would enable them to earn more money.

As for Breadon, he was nearing the end of his life. Two years later, he died of cancer.

10

The New Year saw four contenders for the National League pennant: The Dodgers, the Braves, the Giants, and us. In other words, three teams in the industrial North and the Cardinals out in the Midwest.

That's one of the things I really loved about playing for the Cardinals. Players in New York may have gotten more media exposure than those of other areas, but so many teams fought for fan loyalty and affection in that part of the country. On the other hand, there were no major league teams west of St. Louis in those days. Because the Browns were, for the most part, a losing ballclub, that made the Cardinals the team of the West. Fan loyalty was just tremendous. I received fan mail all the time. It was not unusual for trainloads of people from Illinois, Iowa, and other midwestern states to come watch their beloved Redbirds play ball.

On the other hand, Durocher's suspension was up and he was back as manager of the Dodgers. His fiery manner was quite a contrast to the easygoing manner of Burt Shotton. Furthermore, the Dodgers decided that it was time to establish Robinson, the National League's first official Rookie of the Year, at his best position. The first week in March, Eddie Stanky was sold to the Braves to make room for Jackie at second base. This opened first base for Gil Hodges, who had been a backup catcher.

In addition to Stanky, the Braves were also improving themselves up the middle by bringing up young shortstop Alvin Dark, and manager Billy Southworth was praying for pitching prospects from the club's farm system to give the staff some depth beyond Spahn and Sain.

Meanwhile, Eddie Dyer was also praying for mound help from the Cardinals' farm system. But Dyer also was looking for some help at first base, so that he could move Musial back to the outfield where he could get more use out of The Man's speed and his strong arm. Now, personally, I always felt that Musial was more adapted to first base than the outfield. Don't get me wrong, Musial was a fine outfielder, but I just felt he was more graceful at first base. When he played the outfield, I noticed that he tended to take an extra step after recovering a batted ball before he threw it back in. Every time you take a step in the outfield on a play, the baserunner is taking three steps along the baseline.

But I wasn't the manager. Dyer was, and he wanted Musial in the outfield. He was willing to give Dick Sisler another chance at winning the first base job.

Early in the season, I went to bat 34 straight times without a hit. Writers speculated that I was nearing the end of the line, and that it was time to replace me with a younger ballplayer. To suggestions of that nature, Dyer replied, "I won't bench him because I want to win the pennant. The Cardinals can't win with Slaughter out. The day he's through, he'll know it and so will I. That will be the day he'll have to walk. He's not hitting now, and he didn't hit in spring training. I don't like it, but I'm not irked nearly as much as he is."

Sure, I was irked. But I wasn't discouraged. I said at the time that sooner or later I was going to snap out of it, and some of the pitchers were going to be sorry. I proved myself correct when I hit in 17 straight games from May 3 until May 23. I was 28 for 60 during that streak.

The Cardinals had injuries in 1948 which would lead to the demise of playing careers. Marty Marion still was suffering from back problems. He didn't miss that many games in 1948, but his career was about to take a nosedive because of the bad back.

More immediately affecting us that year was Kurowski's right arm. Whitey had undergone an operation on that arm, but he had obviously lost a lot. Finally, Dyer had to replace him at third base with a journeyman minor leaguer named Don Lang. Lang had last played in the big time for Cincinnati ten years before, but Whitey just couldn't cut it any more, and his power was missed. Finally, a month before the season was out, he had to go back under the knife and have some bone chips removed.

I got a little bashed up myself when I pulled a muscle in my right thigh in Pittsburgh's Forbes Field as I tried to catch a drive off Danny Murtaugh's bat. I also had to have my left forearm bandaged when I slid against some cinders in the Philadelphia bullpen as I prevented a baserunner from advancing to second. For that matter, I had a burn on my thigh the size of a hat from sliding, and my left heel was sore for a while from being spiked. I didn't miss any playing time over these little mishaps. In fact, my team-mates felt that I played better when I had little aches like that to complain about.

Actually, despite my miserable start, I was turning the season into my best year ever. I went on a streak from July 22 until August 8, raising my average to .321, one point higher than I had ever hit in a full season. Then, in late August, I got 20 hits in 36 at-bats to move ahead of Cubs outfielder Andy Pafko and Braves shortstop Alvin Dark to the number two spot in the National League batting race. Well, you couldn't really call it a race at all that season. My teammate Stan Musial jumped way out in front, and stayed there.

The Man went on to have the best season of his great career. What a year it was! He was the obvious choice for Most Valuable Player in the National League that year as he posted career high numbers to lead the senior circuit in batting (.376), slugging (.702), hits (230), runs (135), and runs-batted-in (131). He also led the league in doubles and triples. With one more home run, he would have had 40, enough to tie Mize and Pittsburgh's Ralph Kiner for the league lead, giving Stan the Man a triple crown.

Stan is every bit the nice guy people say he is. He is quiet and unassuming. He would rather let his bat do his talking. And in 1948, it spoke louder than ever.

People sometimes ask me if I ever felt that I lost some personal recognition by having to play in the shadow of such a great ballplayer as Musial. I never felt like I was playing in his shadow.

Every year I was his teammate, I was also a member of the National League All-Star team. All ten of them. I feel that if you are recognized as an All-Star, you don't have to worry about lack of identity. I don't think that the shadows came until later.

On August 10, I stole the spotlight from Bucky Walters as the old pitcher made his debut as the Cincinnati Reds manager at Crosley Field. With my left forearm bandaged from my recent slide on the gravel in the Shibe Park bullpen, I went four-for-four with a double and triple and drove in five runs as Harry Brecheen beat the Reds 6-2.

The Cardinals held a night in my honor on August 31. National League President Ford Frick was on hand along with my wife and kids, my mother, my brother Hayward, and quite a few local dignitaries. I was showered with gifts. Fans, almost 21,000 on hand, had raised enough money among themselves to present me with a brand new Buick Roadmaster. Not to be outdone, the Chevrolet dealers in the area gave me a Cabrolet convertible, and my teammates bought me a movie camera and projector. Among other gifts I received that night were a deer rifle, a deep freeze unit, an outboard motor, a playpen for Patricia, a package of rattlesnake meat, fishing gear, a canary, and flowers from my mother. The St. Louis Post Office Drum and Bugle Corps provided the music, while a local musician named Joseph A. Saracini contributed a song he had written about me called "Enos Slaughter's The Man. "

To a remark stating that I probably would continue with the Cardinals for a long time, I replied: "That suits me just fine. Great outfit, these Cardinals. I love St. Louis as much as I think St. Louis loves me. Never played for any other team since I came into organized ball, and I hope I never do."

Something else I really appreciated that day. Eddie Dyer let me choose who I wanted to be the starting pitcher. I asked him to pitch George Munger.

"He's had a rough year, Skip, and maybe it will help him and the club," I told Dyer. I just felt that the big guy could win for us. I figured a Munger victory would be a big lift not only for him but for the entire club. The Dodgers had just knocked us off in four straight games and we needed a pickup.

Big Red shut the Phillies out that night, fooling them with knuckleballs and then blowing the fastball by them. With two men on base, I made a diving catch in left center which killed the only rally they had. At the plate, I hit the ball hard twice to no avail in my first two trips before singling in Musial in the eighth.

With the 5-0 victory ending our losing streak, sportswriter Bob Broeg was prompted to write, "Maybe there ought to be a Slaughter Night every night."

Despite the recognition Stan and I were getting, 1948 was the year for "Spahn, Sain and pray for rain." This might surprise you if you weren't around to remember it, but it really wasn't one of Warren Spahn's better years. He won only 15 games, modest by his standards, and his 3.71 earned run average that season was the highest of his career until 1964, when he was 43 years old. The 1948 season, however, did turn out to be Johnny Sain's best. He won 24 games and pitched more games and innings than anyone else in the league.

If the Braves prayed for rain before their Cardinals games that summer, it wasn't because they wanted their two best pitchers to face me. I hit close to .500 against both Spahn and Sain and drove in almost thirty runs against that duo.

Dyer's strategy against the Braves that year was the same strategy that other teams used against us: a steady diet of lefthanders. Because their offensive attack included hot-hitting outfielders Tommy Holmes and Jeff Heath, as well as powerful first baseman Earl Torgeson (all lefthanded swingers), we usually went at them with either Harry Brecheen, Howie Pollet, or Al Brazle on the mound. For the most part, this strategy worked.

By September, there was a four team race for the National League pennant. The Dodgers had won 42 out of their last 58 games to rise from last place to contention. The Pirates were the surprise team in the race. Pittsburgh leftfielder Ralph Kiner was still hitting those home runs, but a lot of people were giving credit for the Bucs' success to their rookie manager Billy Meyer, who caught a little for Connie Mack's Philadelphia Athletics around the time I was born. But, Southworth's Braves really caught fire later in September and toward the end there really wasn't a pennant race at all.

Brecheen was our best pitcher that year as he led us to a second place finish with the only 20-victory season of his career. "The Cat" led the league in ERA and winning percentage. Harry may have been small in stature, but he had the heart of a lion. He wasn't afraid to challenge anybody. If a batter took a toehold at the plate, he would cut one loose at him and then holler, "Look out!" By then, of course, it would be too late for the poor guy in the batter's box to get out of the way. This practice may not have earned him too many friends around the league, but, more often than not, it gave him the outside corner.

Unfortunately for the Cardinals that year, we didn't match the Braves in starting pitching. Murry Dickson was once again the guy Dyer used most, but he gave up a record total of 39 home runs and had his second straight losing season. Pollet, despite his 13-8 record, was not the mystery he had been to opposing batters during his earlier years.

Dyer caught a lot of flack for sticking with this pair as much as he did. His detractors alleged that he went out of his way to cater to Pollet along with Red Munger, Ted Wilks and Joffre Cross because they all lived in the Houston area. Well, I'm not from Houston, but I think that Eddie Dyer was as good a manager as I ever played under. To me, he was like a big brother.

Another guy who was like a brother to me, Terry Moore, gave up his centerfield duties and became a full-time coach for the Cardinals near the end of the season. The retirement of my road roomie as a player left me the senior on the team in length of service. Only pitcher Alpha Brazle, who turned 35 right after the season, and 33-year-old relative newcomer Don Lang were older.

For me, the 1948 season ended with a bang. We were playing Boston at Braves Field on September 22. Southworth and his boys had an eight game lead over us, and a defeat for us in that contest would have clinched a pennant for Beantown. It didn't happen that day. We knocked Spahn out of the box before he had a chance to bat.

In the fourth, I got a base hit off former teammate Red Barrett and, with first baseman Nippy Jones at bat, I tore off for second on a hit-and-run. I got such a good jump off Barrett that Buzzy Wares, our first base coach, hollered at Jones, "Let it go."

Upon hearing that command, I turned my head toward the batter's box, anticipating a throw to second from catcher Phil Masi. That turn of my head probably saved my life. Jones hit the ball sharply in the direction of right field. The only reason it didn't make it through was that it collided with my face travelling at 150 miles per hour.

The next thing I remember, I was in the Braves clubhouse with blood-soaked towels over my face. Dr. Richard Gorman, their team physician, asked me if I had ever had a broken nose before. I spent the next couple of days in St. Elizabeth's Hospital and missed the rest of the season. Doctors told me that if I hadn't turned my head, the ball would have struck me in the temple, and I probably would have been killed.

After peaking at .338 in September, I ended up the season with a .321 average, fifth in the league behind Musial, rookie center-fielder Richie Ashburn of the Phillies, and Tommy Holmes and shortstop Al Dark of the Braves. My streak of scoring 100 runs per season was broken at three as I had to settle for 90 that year, to go along with 91 runs-batted-in. I had played every inning of every game before being struck by the line drive. I was glad to be alive, but I had been looking forward to keeping that streak intact for the remainder of the year. Musial had done it two years earlier, in 1946.

One more note about Stan. He tagged the Braves for five hits in the game in which my nose was broken. It was the fourth five-hit game for The Man that year. The last player to get four five-hit games during the same season had been Ty Cobb, all the way back in 1922.

11

The Cardinals lost the 1949 pennant on January 29, when Saigh and Hannegan sold Murry Dickson to the Pirates for $175,000. Murry hadn't done too well the year before and the organization needed the money to pay its taxes, but it turned out to be a move we all would regret.

We were hoping that a hard-throwing Missouri righthander named Cloyd Boyer, who had led the Texas League in strikeouts, was ready to take his place, but the 21-year-old hurler was still a year off, and he never did develop into another Murry Dickson. He did have a kid brother named Ken who would join the organization that year as a pitcher who could swing a mean bat. It was a good thing for Ken and the Cardinals, as it had been for Stan Musial, that they didn't have the designated hitter rule in the minor leagues back then.

I took Terry's place as team captain. Among other things, it meant an additional $500 to my annual salary. I felt that the most important part of being captain was to lead by example rather than tell the other guys what to do. One day, as I was working out before an exhibition game with the Yankees, Casey Stengel, who had just taken over as their new manager, approached me and said: "Take it a little easy, Enos. You're going to embarrass some of my boys."

"Can't do it," I replied. "I'm not made that way."

Of course, I was a "holler guy" on the bench. No matter how far we were down, I always tried to keep the spirit of my fellow Cardinals up and let them know that we had a chance to win. I also didn't mind giving my opponents an earful now and then. Of course, I had done that all along. Showing a little life on the bench kept up the enthusiasm that led to performance on the field. Terry

Moore always liked to point out that I didn't open my mouth during my rookie year with the Cardinals, and that I never shut it after that.

Whitey Kurowski was at the end of his major league career. He was barely 31, but he was losing the battle of the bulge and his arm had gone bad. Later, he would manage in the Cardinals farm system. Don Lang, whom we had picked up the previous year from Cincinnati to help him out, was also finished. In their places were two rookies, Eddie Kazak and Tommy Glaviano.

While Schoendienst and Marion were still in charge up the middle, Nippy Jones was getting some competition at first base from a young lefthanded hitter named Glenn Nelson. Rocky, as the rookie was nicknamed, was considered capable of playing the outfield. So was Glaviano.

What the Cardinals really wanted in their outfield was someone who could hit home runs. One candidate was Bill Howerton, who went by the nickname "Hopalong". Another Cardinal farmhand, Ed Sauer, saw his status in the organization rise as his brother Hank became a major home run hitter for the Cincinnati Reds.

With the vast Cardinal farm system, there were always promising players hungry to emerge from the Chain Gang. I can't remember a year that went by without talk of at least one outfielder at the top level of the farm system who was tearing up his league and itching to replace a veteran. I knew that even though I was a perennial All-Star, I had to work constantly in order to keep my job in the outfield. Management always liked to let me know about the promising minor leaguers they had and to tell me what I knew all along, that it was up to me to keep my job. I knew that if I gave it all I had, there was no way I could be replaced on the field. I told them, "You can bring in all the outfielders you want to, but if one of them beats me out and takes my place, you're going to have one of the greatest baseball teams you ever had."

In addition to hungry young outfielders in the Cardinals Chain Gang trying to replace me, young pitchers kept surfacing around the league whose job it was to make me look bad at the plate. Guys like Robin Roberts of the Phillies or Don Newcombe of the Dodgrs came up and were always looking for new ways to get you out.

Being a hitter in the National League took mental preparation as well as physical work habits. When facing a pitcher, I rarely went after the first pitch. I know it's important to get ahead in the count with the pitcher, but I honestly believe that I was a better hitter with two strikes and no balls than with three balls and no strikes. That's because I knew that I had to make contact, and I didn't try to overswing.

Once again, I won an outfield spot in spring training, but after that I did everything to lose it, at the plate anyway. I just couldn't get a base hit to save my life. Nothing worked. Nothing but a benching by Eddie Dyer.

It must have hurt Dyer as much as it hurt me for him to take me out of the lineup, but that's just what he did during a road trip in May. The sportswriters went on about how all my constant hustling had burned me out at the age of 33. Just as they were predicting the end of my playing career, my manager told them that he was sitting me down.

"I hate to do it, but Country is playing terribly," said Dyer to the beat writers. "Maybe a rest will do him good. I hope so, because we can't win the pennant without him."

That was only the second time I had been benched since Frank Frisch took me out of the lineup for a while during my first year with the Cardinals. And boy, did it hurt. I couldn't eat. I couldn't sleep. I couldn't do anything but wonder when Eddie was going to put my name back on that lineup card.

"The kid isn't through yet," I told anybody who wanted to listen, but it didn't look like I had many believers. So, for four days, I sat and watched helplessly, feeling like a caged animal. And when Eddie opened that cage for me, I took off, playing the best ball of my life.

Stan Musial and I both took a little extra batting practice soon after I had been given my reprieve. He hadn't been doing so well, either. With the Cardinals off to a miserable start, having slumped to seventh place, Dyer arranged for a private session for the two guys he counted on for a lefthanded one-two punch. I took my cuts at pitches thrown by Cloyd Boyer, another pitcher named Ray Yochim and even first baseman Rocky Nelson until my hands were bleeding from the blisters. But the extra practice helped me to find my batting stroke.

The Dodgers were the youngest team in the league that season, with an average age of 26 years. With me as the team's "old man," the Cards' average age was 29. But it was our turn to catch up to Brooklyn. We finally pushed the Bums out of first place in August. After winning the first two games of a series in Flatbush, we took the lead by knocking their sensational rookie Don Newcombe out of the box before he could get a single out. Stan hit for the cycle that day, and finally lifted his average above .300, as we humiliated Brooklyn 14-1 in front of the shocked Ebbets Field fans. I went three-for-six in that rout.

So we were neck and neck with Brooklyn in the pennant race. One highlight for me came on August 9, when I drove in six runs with two homers, including a grand slam off Cincinnati reliever Ken Burkhart, to keep us in a first place tie.

My batting average kept rising. By Labor Day, I had a hitting streak of 12 games. I batted .451 during that streak, and .535 during its last six contests. Over that holiday weekend, we played 52 innings of baseball in a period of 46 hours. We battled the Reds for 15 innings on the night of September 3. That contest was called due to the mandatory 12:50 a.m. curfew in effect at the time, and a double-header was rescheduled for the following afternoon.

Those games were only nine innings apiece, but the next day, we had another double-header scheduled against the Pirates. Pittsburgh wasn't doing too well that year, but they always seemed to give us a run for our money in 1949. The two teams had a running feud going for just about the entire season. It stemmed from an incident at Sportsmans Park when our pitcher Ken Johnson beaned their shortstop Stan Rojek.

We coasted through the first game with them that Labor Day to a 9-1 victory, but the nightcap was a mental and physical grinder. In the second inning, I was on first when Marion grounded to short on a double play ball. I slid into second base with my spikes high. It didn't stop keystoner Danny Murtaugh from turning the double play, but when he saw blood on his chest, the blood still inside of him started to boil. As I entered the dugout, I looked up and there was Murtaugh fuming at me like I had let all of his cows out of the barn.

"If you were an infielder, you wouldn't try to spike a fellow in the chest," he screamed at me (between the cuss words). "Just because you're an outfielder and you can't get run over on the bases, you feel you can take liberties," he raged. "Okay, fellow, you asked for it!"

I never did appreciate this "you're an outfielder" bullshit people tried to hang on me, and I let him know that I would gladly accept his challenge, but as he tossed his glove aside and headed to the dugout, Nippy Jones grabbed Murtaugh from behind and a few of the guys on our bench kept us apart.

Then Pirates manager Bill Meyer started yelling at Dyer. "Do that to the Dodgers, you bums," he hollered.

"Why pick on us? We're not going anywhere," the Bucs' pilot continued. "If that's the way you want to play, we'll play it your way. You've been asking for it all year, and we can give it to you now."

When I led off the eighth, Pittsburgh's tall lefthander Cliff Chambers had entered the game. He had been scheduled to start against Cincinnati the following night, but by this time, Meyer was so fired up that he was willing to throw all his resources against us. The southpaw had two strikes on me, then fired a knockdown pitch at my head. The next pitch came just as fast at my feet, so that I had to skip rope. But the next one he threw, I knocked against the foul pole in right field, and was able to score the tying run when Marion singled.

Finally, though, they beat us in the tenth, with Murtaugh doubling and then scoring on shortstop Stan Rojek's double.

That's really all there was to it. Except that every time I went to Forbes Field after that, the fans would ride me. They'd call me yellow. For that matter, they'd call me everything in the book. It took two or three hits against their pitchers to shut them up.

That was about the only time I ever had fans giving me a hard time, and that didn't last very long. Philadelphia probably had the nastiest fans in baseball at that time, but even those fans never got on me. I think that as long as you were able to get on base and hurt their team, they stayed off you.

It was beginning to look like I had a chance to win both the batting championship and the Most Valuable Player award, which had eluded me in 1942. With two weeks left in the season, I was leading the league with a .342 average. Furthermore, we were ahead of the Dodgers by two games with only five left to be played. Then I slumped. Musial slumped. The whole damned team slumped. And Brooklyn won the pennant.

I finished at .336, third in the league behind Robinson and Musial. Jackie also beat me out for the Most Valuable Player award. I had no quarrel with that. He outhit me at the end, drove in more runs than anyone else, and led his team to the pennant. So, as far as I'm concerned, the writers made the right choice. What I *didn't* appreciate were the articles and columns saying the Cardinals had lost the pennant because "Slaughter had run out of gas."

I did lead the league in triples with thirteen. It was the second time I had led the league in that department. Extra base hits is one area where hustling really pays off. I had learned long before that those extra base hits start with the first four or five steps away from the plate.

One last note about the season in which we lost the pennant by one game. Murry Dickson, that "over the hill" pitcher we sold to Pittsburgh before the season, beat us four times.

12

After batting .336 in my ninth major league season, I signed a contract for $25,000, my highest in baseball. $25,000 was a respectable salary back in 1950, but today, there are ballplayers making more than that for one game.

Pounding the pavement as a coffee salesman, tramping around on my hunting trips, and watching the starches in my diet had helped me to lose nine pounds after the holidays and arrive at spring training weighing 190. That was lighter than any year since I had returned from the service. I wanted to see if I could avoid a slow start like I'd had the previous two seasons. I was tired of getting buried by the press each spring.

When the Cardinals reassembled at Al Lang Field that year, there had been an important change in the outfield. Ron Northey had been traded to Cincinnati for none other than Harry Walker, the man we had given up to get Northey. I figured that we would miss Northey's power but I felt that Walker would be of more all-around help for the team. Harry was an ideal leadoff man because he always seemed to find a way to get on base. He had really been a pest to us when he played for the Phillies. Another advantage that I foresaw from that trade was that, with Northey gone, I would be returned to right field.

Another former Cardinal outfielder was back at Al Lang Field in spring training, but this time Erv Dusak was trying to make the team as a pitcher. After being sent down to Rochester the previous spring, the righthander decided that the mound was his spot if he was going to make it in the major leagues. He had thrown a one-hitter against Buffalo and compiled a respectable record as a Triple-A pitcher.

Nippy Jones was lost to the team for almost the entire 1950 season because of a back operation he'd undergone in the off-season, but there was still reason for us to feel optimistic about first base. There was hope that we could make up for the power we had lost by trading Northey from the bat of Steve Bilko, a chunky 21-year-old.

Bilko busted down fences in his home town of Nanticoke, Pennsylvania, joined the organization in 1945 and hit a ton of home runs wherever they sent him in the farm system. After he hit 34 homers for Rochester in '49, the Cardinals drooled over what his righthanded power could do for their lineup.

Unfortunately, when Bilko arrived for spring training, everybody saw more of him than they expected. Packing 230 pounds on a 6'1" frame, Steve showed up about 15 pounds overweight. He blamed it on the fact that he was a newlywed, just married over the winter, and felt he had to eat all the food his new bride and new mother-in-law put on the dinner table.

Bilko started the season for us, but played like he had eaten the dinner table as well. Soon he was back at Rochester. Nelson had failed to make the club in spring training. That left Musial holding the bag. With Stan the Man covering first base for us, I was back in right field.

Like the beginning of 1939, the start of the 1950 season had a tragic beginning for me. We played our first game in Pittsburgh, and the following day, the game was called on account of snow. Rather than counting on the snow to melt, league officials decided to make up the rest of the series at a later date, so the team got ready to head back to St. Louis for our home opener. Before we boarded the train, my oldest brother Daniel called me from Roxboro with some bad news.

Carlton had been killed in an accident on his farm. His tractor had been stuck in the mud, and he was trying to get it loose by putting it in reverse and then jerking it forward. When the tractor jerked loose, it did so with too much force, and it turned over on him. When he didn't show up for lunch, his wife went looking for him and discovered him crushed to death under the tractor.

Instead of travelling with the team to St. Louis, I caught a midnight flight from Pittsburgh to the Raleigh-Durham Airport, where I was met by my family and driven to Roxboro. Carlton was buried the day before the Cardinals' first home game.

I had left my automobile in Roxboro when I had gone to spring training that year. Since I had been called home by this family emergency, I decided to take the car with me back to St. Louis. I also decided to take mother with me so that she could watch some baseball and, perhaps, keep her mind off this latest family tragedy. At four o'clock in the afternoon of the day of Carlton's funeral, I started driving mother and myself to our destination. I drove all night. We got into St. Louis at ten o'clock the next morning, and I played the home opener at two-thirty that afternoon.

Despite my off-season conditioning, I still suffered an early season slump. By the middle of May, I was only batting around .250. Then, I caught fire. A month later, I had raised my average by almost 100 points and found myself, once again, contending for the batting title.

There was no question that I was a streak hitter throughout my career, but some things about my hitting didn't change. I never altered my batting stance. I stood the same way at the plate from my first season at Martinsville in 1935 until I retired from baseball. And I always stuck with the same style bat, a 35-inch, 34-ounce model with a slim handle and a big knob.

Pitchers around the league respected my ability to hit a fastball and were careful how they pitched to me. They liked to mix up their pitches by feeding me something inside and then something outside. There weren't any pitchers I could really say I owned. But for that matter, there weren't pitchers who consistently put a hex on me, either. If a pitcher horse-collared me in a game, I would usually get him back the next time. Also, I found I would just as soon bat against a veteran I was familiar with as a rookie I hadn't had a chance to take a look at.

But, no matter who the pitcher was, the way I hit wasn't a secret. I just kept swinging and kept running. Once I got a piece of the ball, I ran like hell, no matter whether it was a line shot or a weak dribbler. When an infielder knows you're giving all you've got to get to first base, he's more inclined to rush the throw. And rushing makes for the occasional error.

One thing that really got my goat was watching teammates not bother to run out ground balls. To me that just wasn't the Cardinal style of baseball. Once one of our guys tapped a weak dribbler. When he saw that it was headed straight for the shortstop, he took a few trots, then turned to the dugout. "Why didn't you run it out? That guy at short ain't no wizard," I hollered at him.

"And my name ain't Country Slaughter," he shouted back.

I took that retort as a compliment. Actually, though Country may, to this day, be my best known nickname, few of my teammates ever called me that. Dizzy Dean used to, but Diz was a radio broadcaster instead of a ballplayer by then. I was called Country a lot by the media and the fans, but most of my teammates called me Eno. Another popular nickname for me was Bosco. I really don't know where that one came from, but Bob Broeg of the *St. Louis Post-Dispatch* and Red Schoendienst have always liked to call me that. When I was living in my first suburban home after the war, some local writers liked to refer to me as the "Ferguson Flyer."

Others liked to refer to me as "Old Aches and Pains" because of my habit of talking about my bumps and bruises, but that nickname is better identified with the late Hall-of-Famer Luke Appling, who was playing shortstop for the Chicago White Sox at the time. As my tenure with the Cardinals grew longer, I was more and more being known as The Old Warhorse. During my final years in the big leagues, when I was the oldest player in the game, some of the sportswriters started nicknaming me after my age.

I was also called "The Baker" or "Bake." Just for the hell of it, I started saying to dugout visitors, "I wish I'da known you were coming out today. I'da baked you a cake." I said it over and over, and the saying must have caught on. A young lady named Eileen Barton recorded a song that year called, "If I'da Known You Were Coming I'da Baked a Cake." It became the hottest-selling record in the country.

I may have had a lot of nicknames, but my trademark was hustling. One example of the importance of running out a ground ball occurred on June 1 in a game against Brooklyn, who had come into town a game ahead of us. Robinson doubled off Howie Pollet in the third to put them two up. In the fourth, Preacher Roe had two of us out with two on when I came to bat. I hit a grounder that I thought had a chance to get through to right field, but Robinson made a tremendous stop. Even though it looked like he had me dead in my tracks, I hustled to first at full speed anyway. As it turned out, the throw was a little low and first baseman Gil Hodges momentarily bobbled it. I was safe. Then Marty Marion hit a grand slam home run to put us ahead to stay. The point is, if I hadn't been moving at full speed from the moment I hit the ball, they would have probably gotten me for the third out. But instead, the bases were loaded for Slats to clear.

We won the game, but we lost a lot that day. In the fourth, with a man on, Garagiola bunted to Hodges, who made a quick throw to shortstop Pee Wee Reese. The Dodger captain turned and fired to Robinson, who had broken to first on the bunt so that they could double-up Garagiola. Somewhere between Robinson's hustle to the bag for the extra out and Garagiola's intense drive to avoid the humiliation of a bunt double play, there was a collision at first base. Joe tripped over Jackie, lost his balance and crashed to the ground on his left side.

The Dodger second baseman was shaken up a bit on the play and suffered a bruise on his right calf, but the Cardinals were the big losers in that smashup: Garagiola had a separated shoulder. At first Dr. Hyland announced that we'd only lose Joe for 10 to 14 days, but as it turned out, we didn't get him back until September.

Dr. Robert F. Hyland, the Cardinals team physician, was one of the best doctors in the baseball business. He had taken care of players from way back and had some famous and successful satisfied customers, including Babe Ruth and Frank Frisch. One of his philosophies was that a ballplayer should never be operated on unless it was as a last resort. Considering that surgical technology in the thirties and forties was nowhere near what it is today, I don't believe that was a bad philosophy at all.

After Fred Saigh purchased the Cardinals from Sam Breadon, he didn't like Dr. Hyland for some reason and he quit letting the ballplayers go to see him. One season, our catcher Del Rice had come down with a separated shoulder. The doctors wanted to operate. Del refused to let them cut on him. Against the club's wishes, he went back to see Dr. Hyland. Instead of going under the knife, Del was merely wrapped up in tape. Hyland's method worked. Rice eventually healed and regained his arm strength.

It was Rice who did most of the catching for us the rest of my years with the Cardinals. He may not have hit too well, but he was an excellent defensive catcher. He had a strong, accurate arm, and he seemed to know how to get the most out of the pitchers. His ability to motivate helped him stay in baseball for the rest of his life. He played in the majors for 17 years, and in 1972 he managed the California Angels.

Meanwhile, Garagiola agreed to the club's wishes and underwent shoulder surgery. I think that the operation ended up cutting a lot of years off his playing career, because he never seemed to be able to throw as well after that. Once one of the most highly-regarded catching prospects, Joe ended up bouncing around the league, spending time with the Pirates, Cubs, and Giants before calling it quits at twenty-eight.

I think that trading a catcher's mitt for a microphone was a wise move on Joe's part. He always.had a great sense of humor, even when he was a player. I'm not surprised that he was able to combine his baseball knowledge and his gift of gab and go on to a very successful broadcasting career.

The injury was demoralizing to the club because Joe had always been such a likable guy to have around — and he was finally having a really good year for us, batting a torrid .347 and starting to look like he might be the catcher the Cardinals had hoped for when they sold Walker Cooper. But he never was the same after that operation.

Suddenly, we were plagued with the injury hex. It almost reminded me of 1941. Centerfielder Chuck Diering broke his right elbow. They had to cut into Ted Wilks' right elbow and take out bone chips. All this on top of Nippy Jones' back meant trouble down the road.

Despite injury problems, the Cardinals had a two-game lead on June 12 when we headed out for an 18-day road trip.

Tommy Glaviano improved his hitting to the point that Dyer gave him the third base job over Kazak, who was our primary pinch-hitter that year. Tommy was a kid who loved to play practical jokes on his teammates. This turned out to be his best year, but all was not smooth sailing for the young Californian we called "Bugs Bunny." One game in mid-May, he muffed three straight balls hit to him in a game against the Dodgers, and Brooklyn came from behind to beat us 9-8. In the Ebbets Field clubhouse and on the sleeper train ride to our next game at Boston, the poor guy had none of his happy-go-lucky nature. He looked like he was about to break down crying any minute. The next morning, he was still gloomy as he ate breakfast in the hotel coffee shop and went straight back to his room. As team captain, I thought I'd do what I could to lift his spirits, so I gave him a call.

"Come on, kid. You and I and Terry Moore are going to the movies," I told him over the hotel telephone. "No use for you to sit up there in your room. Tonight's another game."

The movie we went to see was a mystery starring Edmund O'Brien called "D.O.A.", which of course stands for "dead on arrival." A lot of people thought that was getting to be an accurate description of the Cardinals. It sure as hell was an accurate description of Glaviano that day.

Fortunately, as we watched that movie our third baseman came back to life. It sure didn't have a happy ending, but it may have helped that the story was situated in Tommy's home state of California. The film featured some hot jazz, and that also may have perked him up. All I know was that as Sam Bigelow, O'Brien's character in the movie, gradually died, Glaviano came back to life. As we left the theater, Tommy was his old happy-go-lucky self again. That night, as the game was being rained out, instead of moping about how he blew our last Dodgers game, Tommy entertained us with some of his Ink Spots renditions.

Meanwhile, Eddie had to decide whether to leave Glaviano at third or to replace him with Kazak. Our manager worried that if he benched the kid, it would be bad for his confidence. He worried even more that if he put the young man back into the lineup and he fouled up again, it might finish him as a ballplayer.

After watching Glaviano clown around in the clubhouse during that rainout, Dyer figured that it was safe to stick with the young third baseman. I'd say it was, too. Tommy doubled in the five-run inning that won the first game for us, and doubled in the eighth inning of the second game to tie the score.

I led all National League outfielders in the voting for the All-Star team that year. Second to me was Pittsburgh's Ralph Kiner, and directly behind him was Hank Sauer. Burt Shotton, managing the team, complained that the fans had voted him three leftfielders. And that wasn't including Musial, who was selected to start at first base. Shotton knew that Kiner and Sauer were as slow as mules, and the Dodgers manager thought that I had a bad knee.

In 1950, the midsummer classic was held at Chicago's Comiskey park for the first time since the original All-Star game in 1933. Up until just a few minutes before the contest was scheduled to start, Shotton hadn't made up his mind whether to start Sauer or me in center. He approached me about my knee, and I told him it was fine. I told him that I had played center some when I was a rookie in 1938, and that I'd play anywhere he wanted me to.

So I played in center field that day, and Hank started in right. I think that last-minute decision ended up saving the game for the National League. In the second inning Walt Dropo, the giant, muscular up-and-coming first baseman of the Boston Red Sox, hammered a drive that was headed over the center field fence at the 415 mark. I raced back to the wall, and snared it with what was referred to by sportswriters as one of the greatest catches in All-Star history. The ball was barely in the webbing of my glove, and, no offense to Sauer, but I don't think Hank would have been able to rob Dropo of that home run.

Since Terry Moore's retirement following the 1948 season, center field continued to be a trouble spot for the team. Chuck Diering batted .250 and in midseason was replaced by Harry Lowery, whom the club purchased from Cincinnati. "Peanuts," as he was better known, had some fine years as an outfielder for the Chicago Cubs before being traded to the Reds the previous season. At 32, he was having a poor year at the plate, and was being squeezed out of the Reds outfield by younger guys like Bob Usher and Joe Adcock. After Peanuts joined the Cardinals, he became my road roommate and soon one of my best friends on the club.

The Cards lost ground pretty steadily after the All-Star break, and wound up with a 78-75 record, 13 games back. Musial won another batting championship, but other than that, the Cardinals were not so invincible. The Phillies, on the other hand, with out-fielders like Del Ennis and Richie Ashburn and pitchers Robin Roberts and Jim Konstanty, won a pennant race that went down to the wire with the Dodgers.

1950 also saw my first venture into the business world, al-though farming takes many of the same skills to succeed. A nice fellow named John Straub and I opened a jewelry store in Belle-ville, an Illinois town of about 35,000 just southeast of St. Louis. I would really enjoy my life as a suburban jeweler. And the fact that there were plenty of Cardinal fans in Belleville didn't hurt. In fact, one of the items we specialized in was "Cardinal dia-monds."

Still, I contributed more to that store than just being Enos "Country" Slaughter, the ballplayer. When you're engraving somebody's precious jewelry, it doesn't matter what your name is. You can't afford to make a mistake. I did just about all the engraving myself, and got to where I was pretty good at operating that machine. John and I were a good team.

Meanwhile, Mary and I weren't getting along too well any-more. Her parents had come down to our house in Ferguson, and started to get into our affairs. I think that's what broke up our marriage more than anything else. We filed for divorce shortly thereafter. She stayed on in the house, and I moved out.

13

After watching his team drop from contender status to fifth place and the organization's revenue drop by $350,000 from 1949 to 1950, it was Fred Saigh's turn to play Sam Breadon's old role as miser. He wanted to cut the salaries of Howie Pollet, Harry Brecheen, George Munger, Ted Wilks and me by 25 percent. Red Schoendienst was asked to accept $3,000 less for his services.

For me, a 25% cut would have meant a drop of $6,250, down to $18,750 after I had batted .290 and, once again, driven in over 100 runs. *St. Louis Star-Times* sportswriter Sid Keener noted in his column that he had been swamped with letters and phone calls by fans who protested my pay cut. Anyway, I finally settled for a $5,000 cut. And for the rest of my career with the Cardinals, I played for $20,000.

Saigh cut Eddie Dyer, too—right out of baseball. After he was fired, the former pitcher went back to his home in Houston and started an insurance agency. Sid Keener had openly campaigned for me to replace Dyer as manager, but I wanted no part of that. Carl Hubbell, who by then was the Giants' farm director and enshrined in the Hall of Fame, had advised me not to get involved with managing until I was through as a player. That seemed to make plenty of sense to me.

A player did accept the job as manager: shortstop Marty Marion. As a player, Slats was in bad shape with a knee so swollen that he could hardly move. That year, he turned the shortstop duties over to pepperpot Solly Hemus, a 27-year-old lefthanded hitter who had spent the previous five seasons in our farm system, primarily as a second baseman. It's interesting to note that when Hemus retired as a player, he also got a chance to manage the

Cardinals. And look at the team's general manager today: Dal Maxvill, another long-time Cardinal shortstop. I hope Ozzie Smith reads this book.

Sure, I was disappointed that I had to take a cut in salary, but I wasn't about to show it by loafing in spring training. During a game at Al Lang field after I had hustled to first base on a routine groundout to the pitcher, dashed back to the dugout after the play, and sprinted to right field after the inning, a sportswriter hollered to Marty through the chicken wire fence: "Some day, they ought to put Slaughter in the Hall of Fame, for no other reason than as an example of what a player can do for himself by hustling."

"There are a lot of other reasons," my new manager responded. "But you know one thing about Enos: If he ever makes the Hall of Fame, they're going to have to catch him to put him there."

After playing alongside Glaviano and Kazak the previous couple of years, Marion decided they weren't the answer to the third base situation. He first tried a pair of former Philadelphia Athletics, Don Richmond and then Vern Benson, at the hot corner. When they didn't work out, the Cardinals sent Don Bollweg, a first baseman who had played in only ten major league games, along with $15,000 for Yankee Billy Johnson.

Johnson had been the Yankees regular third baseman for several seasons. He was never known for his speed, but he did manage to hit four World Series triples, a feat unsurpassed by anyone. More important to us, he was a good man with the glove.

By May, I was hitting about .350 when I came down with the flu. That knocked me out completely and it was a long time before I got back in the groove. Peanuts Lowery and I carried the club in hitting the first month, then I broke a finger in fielding practice before a game and I was playing hurt again. When my finger got better, my average jumped by 60 points in a few weeks. But, the next thing I knew, Marion decided to put Tom Glaviano in right field, and I was on the bench. I was 35 at the time, a year and a half older than Marion. I read where he had said that I was getting old and that Musial and Schoendienst were the only good ballplayers left on the club. I don't know if he was scared that I was after his job or what, but I honestly feel Marion was doing the team a disservice by experimenting with Glaviano. Tommy's hitting dropped off and his weak arm gave him more trouble in the outfield than he ever had at third. Finally, Marion put Glaviano on the bench and put me back in right field.

When I came back after the All-Star game, I got a terrible skin infection that just made me raw all over from the waist down. It was just murder to put on the uniform and take it off.

Despite all my ailments and benchings, I was going strong at the end of the season, and so was the entire club. Musial won another batting championship with a .355 average and had been able to play regularly the whole season. In 106 games that year, I hit only .281, the lowest average since my rookie season. As an outfielder who played in over 100 games, I was, at .995, fourth in the league in fielding percentage behind the Braves' Willard Marshall, Cincinnati's Lloyd Merriman and Monte Irvin of the Giants.

As it turned out, I was the only outfielder with more than 100 games for the Cardinals that year. Musial played in more games than I, but with extensive use at first, only 91 of his games were in the outfield. My roommate Lowery appeared in the outfield 85 times. Marion believed in variety. Forty-one different men played for the Cardinals that year. The eight Cardinals who played the most averaged only 112 games. These eight "regulars" only averaged 101 games at their normal positions.

I didn't complain about the way I had been used, though. Whenever I played, I always did what the manager wanted me to do because I knew that he would have to answer for it.

In 1951, I made the one, and only one, play in my baseball career based on the color of a man's skin. That player was Monte Irvin of the New York Giants. This man had been a great outfielder for the Newark Eagles in Negro League baseball, and I understand that he almost broke the color line ahead of Robinson. After Jackie had established himself with the Dodgers, the Giants bought Irvin from the Eagles and moved him up to the majors. Soon after that, they did the same with another multi-talented Negro League outfielder named Willie Mays.

Their crowded outfield and the sale of Johnny Mize led to Monte being moved to first base. There he was playing first base with his foot drawn across the bag, just like Robinson's was that day in 1947. You know how I feel; the basepaths belong to the runner. I wasn't going to risk injury to avoid spiking a player whose foot was in my way.

But I did. It didn't even occur to me that Irvin was black until I was almost on the bag. But suddenly, it hit me—all the flack I had caught because I'd stepped on Jackie Robinson. So I dove out of the way at the last moment, and fell sprawling to the ground.

"Monte," I said, as I was picking myself up, "if you're going to play first, you'd better learn to give the baserunner some of that bag."

I almost sprained my ankle just to get out of an opponent's way. And that's the only time Enos Slaughter ever did anything like that on a ballfield. But I just didn't want to be in the headlines again on account of a man's color.

Of course, the 1951 National League season ended with the famous "shot heard round the world," Bobby Thompson's 3-run homer to defeat the Dodgers 5-4 in the rubber game of the Giant-Dodger playoff series. But, though losers that year, Brooklyn was building a real dynasty. Catcher Roy Campanella would be the MVP that year. Now, Campanella was always nice to everybody. One thing about him, though, when he was working behind the plate, he'd want to start a conversation with me every time I came up to bat. That was more than just being nice. It was being crafty. He wanted to break my concentration. With the quality pitchers the Dodgers had, I needed to be thinking about the pitcher, not whatever pleasantries Campy wanted to discuss. Sometimes, I'd answer his questions, but I made sure I was ready to hit.

Don't get me wrong. I don't hold his friendliness against the man. Roy was just trying to win ballgames. And I'll say this. Campanella never tried to show anybody up.

Neither did Don Newcombe. Newk, another former Newark Eagle, had joined the Dodgers in 1949 and quickly established himself as a premier major league pitcher. On the mound, he was a real competitor. I hit the dirt plenty of times to get out of the way of fastballs he fired at my head. Did I ever charge the mound after one of his dusters? Hell, no. Sure, he was knocking me down intentionally, but I understood that was just part of the game.

I met my fourth wife after the 1951 season, while I was on a barnstorming tour with some other major leaguers that sent us westward out into California. She was an actress doing bit parts in sketches at theaters out there, and went by the stage name of Vickie Van. My separation from Mary had resulted in another divorce, and Vickie and I saw more and more of each other. I guess I must really believe in marriage, because it wouldn't be too long before Vickie became Mrs. Slaughter.

14

By the beginning of the 1952 season, Marty Marion was still a major leaguer in St. Louis, but no longer with the Cardinals. Fred Saigh had given him his pink slip after the 1951 season, but he caught on with the Browns as a player coach. By June, he was to succeed Rogers Hornsby as manager for the American League club, but his Marty Merry-Go-Round style of baseball was out with the Cardinals.

I carried no grudges against Marty for not using me more. In fact, I told the press I thought he'd done a good job leading us into third place, despite the fact that we had 23 injuries.

Once again, the new manager was younger than I. And for the first time in my career, I was under a playing manager. Frankie Frisch had been a playing manager for the Cardinals, but he had hung up his spikes in 1937, the year before I made it to the big leagues. The only other playing manager I would have was to be myself, but that was still eight years off.

Like Frisch, who had gone to the Hall of Fame in 1947, this man had been the regular second baseman of the New York Giants before being picked up by the Cardinals and appointed manager. Unlike Frisch, this keystoner did not cost the club a superstar like Rogers Hornsby. We had sent Max Lanier and Chuck Diering to the Giants for him at the previous winter meetings.

The new manager was none other than Eddie Stanky, whom I had roughed up on a few occasions while plowing into second.

People wondered how I would be able to get along with Stanky considering that, like Marion, he was younger than I. And was there a possibility he might carry grudges over our collisions on the diamond? I maintained, as I always had, that I could play for anybody. "I always tried to beat Ed Stanky before, but I'll try just as hard to win for him now," I told the media. "He's my type of fellow, always hustling and scrapping."

I'll say this for Eddie Stanky. He could dish it out, and he could take it. If you played rough against him, he wouldn't let you know that it bothered him. A lot of guys dish it out, but then, they can't take it.

One thing that stands out in my memory of Stanky as a manager was the way he liked to give out little fines. If a batter took a third strike, Stanky would fine him a couple of dollars. If a hitter didn't drive in a runner from third, with less than two out, it would cost him a dollar or two. He'd also fine a batter who couldn't sacrifice a runner to second or third a dollar. Considering the salaries major leaguers make today, one laughs at the paltry size of the fines, but you have to remember that this was going on back in the days when a dollar bill was still enough money to mean something.

As far as I'm concerned, there is no place in baseball for that kind of stuff. A lot of players did a lot of things they ordinarily wouldn't do, just so they wouldn't lose a couple of dollars. I don't feel that it helped them to do a better job.

That season Stanky collected $1,455 from the players in fines. He took the money and had a party at the hotel when the season was over. Of course, everyone showed up at the party, because we all had some money invested in it. Solly Hemus had the most, about $85, I think. I contributed a few dollars myself, but not much. Still, I didn't like the idea at all.

There were still some people who thought I should have been named manager of the Cardinals before Stanky, but I still believed in Carl Hubbell's advice and had no designs on the job at the time. I still figured that I had four or five years left as an outfielder. When Marion was fired, I took myself out of the running to be his successor from the very beginning. I did have my own candidate: Terry Moore. But I didn't press the issue; that was Mr. Saigh's business. My business was to do the best I could for whomever he picked.

The team did keep Terry on as a coach. And two years later he managed half a season for the Philadelphia Phillies. That was the only chance he had, but I believe to this day that he would have made a great manager if a major league team had stuck with him.

When I reported for spring training three days early on February 21, Stanky told me that I could take a couple of days off to vacation on the beach, but I was ready to go to work. I couldn't wait to begin those workouts and get into those pepper games.

I soon found more to like about my new manager. From his training system, it was obvious that we were going to be a running club, just like the old Cardinals had been. I know that taking that extra base won us a lot of ball games, and I felt that we were going back to the style of baseball that would do it for us.

Another thing that gave me a good first impression of Stanky as a manager was the fact that he held only one workout instead of two, as Marion had. I felt that if a player worked hard in the hot Florida sun in the morning, he would really be dragging his tail if he got back out there in the afternoon. I agreed with Eddie that one four-hour workout was enough.

That didn't mean a player should let up during those workouts. I would put a rubber suit on under my uniform and sweat so much that the perspiration was actually running out of my shoes. One writer said my uniform would get so wet during our workouts that it looked like I had dunked myself in Tampa Bay.

I didn't mind admitting to the writers that these workouts drained me of some energy. "Sure, I'm tired. Dog tired," I told them. "But it's the only way I know of to get into condition and be able to give all you've got when the real ball games begin. By being tired now, I'll be able to go all the way later on and it will never bother me."

At first, it appeared to many that Stanky also would insert himself in the lineup and move Schoendienst over to shortstop. I didn't think that was a particularly good idea because I didn't feel that Red had the arm to play short. Solly Hemus didn't think it wise either, and he showed up in Florida three days early like I did to prove it. Meanwhile, Stanky started off spring training with the flu, and by the time we were ready to go north, Solly had held on to his shortstop position, Red stayed at second and Stanky had relegated himself to the bench.

Schoendienst was also named co-captain. Sharing that position with Red was okay with me. What I didn't want to share was my position in rightfield. Just because I was about to turn 36 didn't mean I was ready to be sent out to pasture.

"What is wrong with present day ballplayers?" I asked a group of writers one day at Al Lang Field. "Why don't they last longer? Cobb, Speaker and Ruth all played big league ball until they were past forty. Why, they tell me Old Man Wagner was 43 when he quit, and could have gone on for a few more years. Just why is a present day player supposed to be all washed up when he passes 35?"

Herb Gorman and Jan Van Loy were outfield candidates looking to take playing time away from me in right field. Steve Bilko was having a good spring at first base, so that meant Musial would probably be the everyday leftfielder. And Wally Westlake, with his much-needed righthanded power, figured to be a fixture in center. Excited about the potential of Gorman, Van Noy and my roommate Peanuts Lowery, Stanky estimated that I'd only be used in 95 or 100 games.

Still, my relationship with my new boss was off to a great start. He paid me a fine compliment at the end of spring training. During our last game in St. Petersburg, Stanky charged into second baseman Gil McDougald and pushed his hand under the Yankee keystoner's wrist in an effort to knock the ball loose. McDougald held on to tag Stanky and throw to first completing the double play, but then he started hollering at our manager for what he had tried to do.

After the game, Stanky was livid.

"All that other league wants to do is cry and bellyache," he complained. He went on reiterating his point before concluding with, "Give me a guy like Country Slaughter any time. If he thinks he's been mistreated, he doesn't say a word. He just gets even the next time. I know."

I scored the winning run in our first regular season game under Stanky, but the club was soon mired in a slump and falling way back behind the Dodgers and Giants. Other than Gerry Staley and a strong bullpen, the pitching staff had early season problems.

Westlake and Bilko also got off to a disappointing start. That led to a trade in June with Cincinnati in which Westlake was swapped for Dick Sisler. After a five-year absence from the Cardinals, Hall-of-Famer George Sisler's son finally became our regular first baseman. Musial moved from left field to replace Westlake in center, and Peanuts Lowery, who had been doing a great job for us as a pinch-hitter, was inserted into left.

That's when the team started to take off. Musial and I really got hot as the temperature went up. The Cubs' Gene Hermanski had the early lead in the All-Star voting, but by mid-June I had overtaken the former Dodger and wound up being selected to start in my tenth consecutive midsummer classic.

I think it surprised a lot of people that I had improved dramatically over the year before, when I had spent so much time on the bench. It certainly quieted talk that I couldn't play for Stanky, or that I was on my way out.

I collected 5 runs-batted-in on June 23, extending my hitting streak to 23 games.

On July 1, I went into our game against the Reds at Sportsmans Park needing four RBI's to reach a lifetime 1,000. In the first inning, with Schoendienst on first, I hit one out off Ken Raffensburger. Then in the seventh, I homered off Phil Haugsted, and it was celebration time. After I got back to the dugout, Stanky ordered me back out to acknowledge the cheers of the excited St. Louis fans. Only Bob Elliot, who had been able to continue playing throughout World War II, had more RBI's in the National League. Then a reserve for the Giants, the former Pirate and Brave outfielder and third baseman had a total of 1,121. My old teammate John Mize had more National League RBI'S, but he was now in the American League as a pinch-hitter and backup first baseman for the Yankees. Not counting Ted Williams, who was flying for the Navy in Korea, Red Sox infielder Vern Stephens was the only other active major leaguer who had driven in more than 1,000 runs at the time. Before I retired, I ended up passing Elliot and Stephens in that category.

Another good thing about that game is that by beating Cincinnati, we stopped Raffensberger's jinx over our rookie pitcher Wilmer "Vinegar Bend" Mizell, a big lefthander. After watching him pitch that night, plate umpire Dusty Bogess said he was the "fastest pitcher in the league." Mizell, a Mississippi-born rookie, had grown up in North Carolina. Despite the zip in his fastball, he was a victim of control problems at the beginning of the season, but he appeared to be learning fast.

That was a good thing, because the Cardinals really needed some young blood on their pitching staff. Harry Brecheen, at 37, was in his last year with the Cardinals, and Max Lanier had already gone to the Giants in the Stanky deal. A lot was needed from Mizell, Cloyd Boyer and Joe Pesko.

There were times when Boyer looked good, and other times he couldn't seem to get anybody out, but one thing that Missouri boy from the big baseball family could do was pick runners off base. During a two week period in June, he picked four runners off second.

The insertion of Lowery into the regular lineup gave Stanky more opportunities to use himself as a pinch-hitter, and he did a good job in that capacity. He had been a regular second baseman for nine years, having served the Cubs, Dodgers, Braves and Giants. Before the season he had every intention of playing at least 100 games for us in 1952. But with Solly Hemus having a good year at shortstop and Red Schoendienst already established as one of the best second basemen in the game, our new manager had seen the handwriting on the wall and stayed on the bench.

Even though the team won eight more games than we had the year before, we had to settle for third behind the Dodgers and Giants.

Surprised that I had become a .300 hitter again, the writers named me Comeback Player of the Year. It's the only award I ever got from the writers, and it's not one that I really wanted. I was in Honolulu at an exhibition game when I found out that I had been voted to receive this so-called honor. I said, "As far as I'm concerned, I've never been any place. If Marty Marion had let me play in 1951, I think I could have hit .310."

I was becoming more and more active in Belleville. During the season that year, I had been initiated into both the local Elks lodge and the Eagles club. I also served on the county draft board.

Business continued to be good for John and me at our jewelry store in Belleville. So good, in fact, that on December 1, we opened a gift shop next door. Red Schoendienst, Joe Garagiola and Larry Ciaffone, an outfielder who had been brought up to St. Louis for a cup of coffee, were nice enough to help out their old teammate by showing up at the grand opening of the Slaughter-Straub gift shop. While the men got a chance to talk baseball with some of the Cardinals, the first four hundred females to make a purchase were given an imitation pearl necklace.

Too bad ballplayers weren't wearing necklaces like they do today. Maybe I could have sold some to Red, Joe and Larry. Of course, I'm not in the jewelry business anymore, but to me necklaces just don't look right on baseball players. I know these fellows make a lot more than players of my day did, but isn't wearing a uniform good enough? What do they have to prove by having strands of gold dangling around their necks while they're chasing around the field? One of these days somebody's going to choke himself sliding into a base or diving after a ball.

15

In 1953, Stanky returned as manager, as did most of the team, though we had a few youngsters come up from the farm system.

After trying to break in for five years, Steve Bilko finally became our regular first baseman. He was a big fellow with some power, but boy, did he strike out a lot. Our rookie third baseman, Ray Jablonski, hit 21 homers, just like Bilko, but had half the strikeouts.

The promotions of Bilko and Jablonski led to the exits of Dick Sisler, Tom Glaviano and Billy Johnson. Peanuts Lowery, however, remained a valuable member of the club, despite the fact that he was replaced in center field by another power-hitting rookie named Rip Repulski. No longer a regular, Lowery was used more than ever as a pinch-hitter, going to bat 59 times under those circumstances. He would deliver 22 hits in those 59 at-bats, enough to lead the league in that category for the second straight year.

We opened the season at the still unfinished Milwaukee County Stadium, the new home of the Braves. A full house of 34,357 fans showed up to welcome their new heroes. Cold weather greeted them, too. It was only 36 degrees that day in the Wisconsin city along the Great Lakes. Sleet came and went all through the first five innings. The fans didn't seem to mind the bad weather. They were just glad to see major league baseball in their hometown, after an absence of 52 years. Pop flies, foul balls, just about anything that happened on the field that day drew roars from the ecstatic crowd.

The pitchers were most deserving of cheers from the fans, at least for the first few innings. Gerry Staley gave up an unearned run in the second, but he was doing a great job that day. The great lefthander Warren Spahn had a no-hitter going in the fifth, when he walked me to open the inning. He tried to pick me off, but the ball got by first baseman Joe Adcock and I moved up to second. The crowd cheered.

Then our rookie third baseman Ray Jablonski lined a clean single to right, and ended the no-hitter and the shutout with one blow. As I crossed the plate with the first visiting run in County Stadium history, I still heard fans shouting with glee. Sure, the Milwaukee fans were delighted to have major league baseball, but I think that the Cardinals being the team of the West for all those years had something to do with it.

Don't get me wrong. These Milwaukee fans were for the Braves. They especially yelled for rookie centerfielder Billy Bruton, who had been an exciting player for the Milwaukee Brewers when they were the Triple-A farm team of the Boston Braves. Bruton could hit and steal a base, but he wasn't much of a home run hitter, so I wasn't playing him that deep. But in the eighth he hit a ball that got into the wind and flew over my head for a triple.

Bruton wound up scoring that inning, but my roommate Peanuts Lowery tied the game in the ninth with a pinch-hit double.

When Bruton came up to bat in the tenth, I was playing deeper in right field than two innings before. Once again, Bruton hit a fly to right-center that got into the wind. This one was headed just to the top of the fence. At the edge of the fence stood excited fans from the overflowing, sellout crowd. With the game on the line, I rushed to the wall and leaped after the speeding baseball. I had the ball in the tip of my glove, but, at that point, things quickly fell apart. One fan knocked the ball out of my glove. Another one grabbed my cap. And the outfield fence bloodied up my elbow.

The umpire calling the play was Lon Warneke. That's right, the same Lon Warneke who pitched for the Cardinals and hit baseballs to me in practice right after I first came up to St. Louis. Warneke thought the ball had bounced over the fence and ruled it a ground rule double. Charlie Grimm flew out of the Braves dugout raising hell. This time it worked for the Braves manager.

Warneke's call was overruled and Bruton was awarded a game-winning home run.

I made the All-Star team for the tenth straight year and went on to have the best performance of my life in such a contest. It was July 14 at Crosley Field, and Pee Wee Reese and I almost singlehandedly beat the American League. I got two hits, drove in two runs, scored once and stole a base. In the sixth inning, I made a diving catch of a ball hit by Detroit Tigers shortstop Harvey Kuenn. That catch still makes the highlight films.

Pee Wee, who had appeared in ten previous All-Star games without a hit, broke out of his slump that day by driving in two runs with a single and a double. The diminutive Dodger shortstop ended up with the only extra base hit of the game.

Reese and the Dodgers ended up having another great season that year, and again won the pennant. Reese hit 13 homers, not bad for a shortstop, but his total didn't scratch the surface of the team's awesome home run power that year. Centerfielder Duke Snider (42 homers), catcher Roy Campanella (41 homers and a league-leading 142 RBI'S, which helped earn him the Most Valuable Player award for the third time in five years), and first baseman Gil Hodges (31 homers) combined with rightfielder Carl Furillo, the batting champion that year (.344 with 21 homers) to power the Dodgers to another pennant.

We finished 22 games back, tying the Phillies for third. I batted .291 and hit only six home runs. Schoendienst hit .342 that year, the highest of any Cardinal. He even hit 15 home runs, more than twice what he'd ever done before. Red didn't let that high average or home run total get in the way of his personality. He was the same every day. Nobody ever had to worry about what kind of mood the man was in. He'd just get the job done, and that was that.

In the World Series, the Dodgers were unable to prevent the New York Yankees from winning their unprecedented fifth consecutive World Championship.

After the Series, Yankee pitcher Ed Lopat, who had compiled the lowest ERA (2.42) in the American League that year, asked me to join a group of All-Stars he was getting together to tour the

Far East. I played center field for the team because Hank Sauer of the Cubs was in left field and Jackie Jensen of the Boston Red Sox was in right. The infield consisted of Eddie Robinson from the Philadelphia Athletics at first base, Nellie Fox of the Chicago White Sox and the Yankees' latest World Series hero Billy Martin at second, the Braves' Eddie Matthews at third and Harvey Kuenn and Pee Wee Reese at short. Yogi Berra was behind the plate. The pitching staff was composed of Robin Roberts and Curt Simmons from the Phillies, Bob Lemon and Mike Garcia from the Cleveland Indians and, of course, Lopat.

We started out in Colorado Springs and went on to Denver, where we played in front of 23,000 people. From there we flew to San Francisco, and then on to Honolulu, where we stayed for ten days.

From Hawaii we flew to Tokyo to begin four weeks in Japan. We averaged over 36,000 spectators a game in this country we had been at war with barely eight years before. Instead of playing on grass, we often wound up playing on fields of volcanic ash. The ball fields there weren't bad, but the ash would stick to our shoes. Another thing about playing in Japan, they would never stop a game on account of rain. I suppose that, after all they had been through, a little water wasn't much of a problem.

Even in those days, I noticed that Japan had some great ball players. There were a few pull hitters, but most of them hit to the opposite field.

The Japanese people really gave us the royal treatment that fall. They literally rolled out the red carpet for us when we first landed at the airport in Tokyo. Then we paraded. Each Ed Lopat All-Star had a convertible of his own to ride in, with our names printed on each side in both English and Japanese. As we paraded from the airport to downtown Tokyo, we threw out trinkets, such as caramel candy, to the crowd. It was estimated that about two million people turned out to see us in that parade. And if I saw two million people, I must have seen two million cameras, because it seemed like every fan I saw had a camera around his neck.

We really enjoyed the special treatment the people lavished upon us while we were over there. As we were being introduced before the games, a beautiful lady always came out and presented us with bouquets of flowers.

After going on to Okinawa to play an American team for a couple of weeks, we took a Philippine Airlines plane to Manila, where we faced a Japanese team that had beaten us in Tokyo, our only loss on the tour.

I can still remember that we played that game under a big black cloud that neither caused rain nor blocked out the sun. It was so damned hot and humid that I could see the perspiration running through my shoes. Bob Lemon had a shutout going for us in the fifth inning, when he fell off the mound because of the heat. Lopat came in and held them scoreless, giving us a 1-0 victory.

The trip back was the least enjoyable part of the tour. First, they said that we had too much baggage to fly back with us on the plane. We had to send most of our belongings by boat, and I got back to the United States a month before my luggage made it home. Furthermore, the plane developed an oil leak, and we had to stop in Guam for four hours while the problem was being repaired. The delay caused us to miss our connections in Honolulu, but we finally made it back to Los Angeles.

Things were changing in St. Louis. The Anheuser-Busch Company, makers of Budweiser and other popular beers, had purchased the Cardinals in 1953. Though that merger would prove to be a lasting one, my days with the Cards were numbered. I didn't realize it then, of course. On December 28, president Gussie Busch signed me for the 1954 season. At the signing he said to me, "You're a credit to the game, and you'll always be with me."

Finally, I got to Florida, where I could work to retain my job in right field. I was about to turn 38, and the "old man" talk continued, but it didn't bother me, because I had been called that ever since I came back from the war.

Times sure had changed in the way the Cardinals were being run from the days when I first came up with the organization. Before I left for the Air Force, Branch Rickey, one of the most knowledgeable and shrewd minds in the history of the game, had run the team. Now that Anheuser-Busch had bought the team, Dick Meyer, a career brewing executive, suddenly found himself in the position of general manager of a baseball team. As far as I'm concerned, he didn't know baseball from a china cabinet.

Two guys in particular were giving me competition for my spot in the outfield that spring. One was Joe Frazier, a journeyman, who had only played nine games in the major leagues. Those had been with Cleveland, back in 1947. The other challenger was Wally Moon, a wiry young outfielder from Arkansas who had played some college ball at Texas A & M. Even though both of these outfield prospects displayed potential for power, I wasn't bothered about the situation.

Despite our finishing 22 games behind the Dodgers in 1953, Meyer had stayed clear of any major trades over the winter. It was obvious the pitching staff needed some help in the starting rotation to complement veteran Gerry Staley and youngsters Harvey Haddix and "Vinegar Bend" Mizell. Then, at the beginning of spring training, we purchased Vic Raschi from the Yankees. Raschi had been the Yankees' most effective pitcher since World War II and, though he was about to turn the ripe old age of 35, he had won thirteen games while losing only six for the world champs the preceding year. It was a turnabout for the Cardinals to pick up an established player for cash. Under the regimes of Breadon and Saigh, it had always been the other way around. Seeing a name player join us rather than go out the door was a positive sign for me. But, I wasn't aware that the other shoe was about to drop.

I had a great spring in Florida that year. As we headed northwest from St. Petersburg, I was looking forward to a good season. I was in top shape. I was excited about the Cardinals' chances against the Dodgers and other NL clubs now that we had added Vic Raschi to our pitching staff.

We arrived in St. Louis for our annual weekend pre-season series with the Browns. It would be the last one because, as it turned out, the Browns were not long for St. Louis.

Neither was I.

In the first game, I doubled off Bob Turley to beat the Browns. That turned out to be my last hit in a Cardinals uniform.

We were losing the Sunday game 8-1 and I was not in the lineup. Along about the seventh or eighth inning, Stanky walked the length of the bench to where I was sitting.

"Slaughter, you can go ahead and get dressed," he said. "The general manager would like to see you in his office."

As I was changing into my street clothes, it honestly didn't occur to me that I was taking off a St. Louis Cardinals uniform for the last time. Coming off a great spring, I actually had the thought that maybe August Busch had decided to give me a raise. So I strolled up to Dick Meyer's desk completely unprepared for the news I was about to receive.

"Eno, all good things must come to an end," Meyer said. "We've traded you to the New York Yankees."

Those words shocked me as much as anything that ever happened to me. The trade caught me totally by surprise. I may have had marriages come and go, but I always thought that I would be able to retire in a Cardinals uniform. Hadn't Busch just told me that I'd always be with the Cardinals? Hadn't I just won another game for them?

I'd broken a collarbone chasing a fly ball in the outfield. I'd been hit by baseballs going 100 miles an hour. But no injury on the field ever caused as much pain as the stabbing sensation in my chest as Meyer said those words. When a pitcher nailed me with his fastball, I never changed expression, rubbed the bruise or did anything to show I had been hurt. But I was no match for the news that the beer executive who was trying to run a baseball team had just delivered to me. Tears gushed from my eyes like water from a broken pipe.

That's when I found out what a cold and heartless game baseball really could be. Just because I was pushing 38, the team that I felt was a part of me had decided I was washed up.

"I'll still be playing in the major leagues when all these other fellows on the Cardinals are gone," I told Meyer.

That didn't quite turn out to be true, but then again, I wasn't too far off. By the time I eventually returned to the National League with the Milwaukee Braves, only one of my former Cardinal teammates was still with the team—Stan Musial. And he might also have been traded had not Busch stepped in and nixed the deal after Stan threatened to retire.

As I got ready to leave the scene of my execution and pack my things to join Casey Stengel in New York, Meyer said, "We've got a news conference set up for after the game. We want you to come back and face the media with us."

"I've got nothing to say," I replied. "You are the ones who did the trading. Go ahead and hold it yourself." But, despite the state of shock I was in, I changed my mind and agreed to meet the press corps.

At this point my ex-manager was not very high in my esteem. I believed that Stanky had been at the bottom of this. "The Brat," as he had been nicknamed during the early days of his playing career, was the only one in Cardinals upper-management with baseball experience. People have told me otherwise, but in my heart I truly feel that Meyer and Busch were too inexperienced to go through with such a deal before consulting him.

Still, I joined him up in Meyer's office for the press conference. Meyer announced that I had been traded to the Yankees for outfielder Bill Virdon, pitcher Mel Wright and Wayne Tellinger. The press immediately speculated that the trade was part of the Raschi deal, but this was steadfastly denied.

Stanky said a few words, and then it was my turn to speak.

"This is the biggest shock of my life," I sobbed in front of the reporters and the cameras.

I eventually calmed down and made it with my baggage to the parking lot, but I ran into Stan Musial and I broke down once again. We had spent a lot of years together in the heart of the Cardinals lineup and it was really sad for both of us to know that our one-two punch had been broken up.

From St. Louis, I flew to Washington, where the Yankees traditionally played the first game of the year against the Senators.

Needless to say, the Yankees were quite different from the team I had faced in the 1942 World Series. For the most part, the names were different, but, unlike the Cardinals, the winning tradition was still there. The only player from that World Series who was still active for the Yankees by the time I joined them was shortstop Phil Rizzuto. Catcher Bill Dickey and third baseman Frank Crosetti, whom I had played against in 1942, were in the midst of long careers as Yankee coaches following their playing days with the club.

During my first tour of duty with the Yankees, I stayed at the Concourse Plaza, only three blocks away from Yankee Stadium. Isn't that something? "Country" Slaughter living in a New York City hotel!

Actually, I didn't mind that nearly as much as I did the fact that I wasn't playing every day. In addition to Mickey Mantle, the centerfielder who was the most exciting young player in the American League at the time, there were three other outfielders who were more than capable of being regulars for just about any other major league club. Both Hank Bauer and Gene Woodling had hit over .300 for the World Champions, and a lefthanded hitter named Irv Noren was reaching his peak.

I had been an All-Star for the previous eleven years as an outfielder for the Cardinals, and I had built up quite a following in the Midwest. But now that I had joined the Yankees, a team of superstars that had won the last five World Series, I felt like I was just another ballplayer. I knew I needed to prove myself all over again.

The way the season started, I wasn't getting a lot of chances to prove to the team what I was worth. Casey went with Bauer most of the time in right field. This tough, stocky ex-Marine had grown up across the river from Sportsmans Park in East St. Louis, Illinois, and, in his childhood, young Hank had followed the Cardinals of Medwick, Martin and Frisch. By the time I reached the Cardinals in 1938, he was 15 years old. Before he went off to war, I understand that he had become quite an Enos Slaughter fan. After earning a Purple Heart fighting the Japanese, he joined the Yankees organization. A big leaguer since 1948, Bauer, like me, was an aggressive ballplayer, one who played to win.

Casey used me mostly as a pinch-hitter and spot player that year. I wasn't happy sitting on the bench, so I went to him and said, "Casey, I'd like to play more."

The Old Professor replied, "My boy, you play when I want you to play and you'll be here for a long time." What could I say? As it turned out, he was right. I was still playing for the Yankees five years later when I was 43 years old.

My former Cardinal teammate Johnny Mize had been with the Yankees, and for that matter, was the American League's top pinch-hitter three years running. By the time the Big Cat decided to hang them up, he had been replaced at first base primarily by the lefthanded-hitting Joe Collins.

Just before I had joined the club that spring, the Yankees decided to bring up a quiet, muscular guy named Bill Skowron, who had been a halfback for the Purdue football team before spending three years in the Yankee farm system. Moose's career got off to a great start as he platooned with Collins that year. Batting primarily against southpaws, he was a tough out. The opposition couldn't tell where he would hit the ball. He'd look to left field, and hit a line drive to right.

The rest of the Yankee infield was having its problems that year. Second baseman Billy Martin, who had been the Most Valuable Player in the last World Series, had been drafted into the army during the off-season. Andy Carey, who was expected to become the new regular third baseman, came down with a torn muscle. And the team's senior player in length of service, Phil Rizzuto, was starting to lose some of his range at short.

Rizzuto had been a great ballplayer his first ten years with the club. You can't take that away from him. But, at 35, he was also having a bad year at the plate, and his days as a regular were numbered. Still, he was a great guy to have on the club. His presence was a boost to the team's morale because he was always fun to play tricks on. I enjoyed watching him raise hell after I spit tobacco juice on his shoes, but that didn't bother him nearly as much as some of the other stunts that were pulled on him. It used to be that players left their gloves on the field while their team was at bat. Sometimes a player would sneak a fishing worm into a finger of Scooter's glove as it lay out there left of second base. When he returned to his shortstop position, right after he slid his fingers into that glove, you would see it fly ten feet into the air.

His vulnerability to practical jokes helped keep us loose. I think, though, that deep down inside, Rizzuto enjoyed all the friendly pranks we pulled on him. But he didn't enjoy sitting on the bench and watching more and more playing time go to Willie Miranda, the 28-year-old Cuban who was on his fourth American League club and would soon be sent to his fifth.

In Martin's absence, the keystone position was being divided between Jerry Coleman and Gil McDougald. Coleman wasn't much of a hitter by then, but I thought he was a very good second baseman. He had a good, quick throw to first and, in my opinion, could turn a double play as easily as anybody. McDougald, who had played more third base during his first three years with the Yankees, was definitely the better hitter of the two.

With McDougald filling in at second and Carey out with a muscle tear, Bobby Brown was getting some playing time, but everybody knew that the 29-year-old med student was going to retire from baseball to complete his internship on July 1. Years later, after a successful career as a physician, he would return to baseball to become president of the Texas Rangers. He is now president of the American League.

Anyway, after Brown retired, Carey came back and had a great season for us. Andy became known for his cockiness and his tremendous appetite, but the thing I'll always remember about Andy Carey is that he threw the heaviest ball I ever caught. We used to warm up together a lot, tossing each other the ball on the field before games. His throws seemed to tear my hands to pieces when I caught them. It's not that he threw so hard, but in some way, when he threw the ball, it seemed like a large rock hitting your hand.

At that time, Yogi Berra was the best catcher in the league. In fact, that year and the next, he was the best *player*, bar none. The baseball writers honored him as the American League's Most Valuable Player in both 1954 and 1955. He had previously received this award in 1951. He was a great bad-ball hitter, and was good for at least 25 home runs every year.

Being teammates with Yogi, I got to know him as a steady personality day in and day out. He might not have said all those

"Yogiisms" that the writers liked to attribute to him, but he was like an old shoe. He had his routines that he went through. Being around him was the same day after day.

The pitching staff was an excellent mixture of youth and experience. Whitey Ford, a native New Yorker like Rizzuto, was at 25 in his third season and steadily establishing himself as one of the best hurlers in the game. That year, though, it was another young New Yorker who stole the excitement. Righthander Bob Grim used his blazing fastball to win 20 games and receive the American League Rookie of the Year award.

Grim's roommate, Allie Reynolds, an American Indian from Oklahoma, had been a great Yankee pitcher for eight years, but by now, he was at the end of the line due to a back injury sustained in a bus accident the year before. His back was still bothering him and he was, at 39, the only player on the team older than me that year. Still, if we needed a win, he'd go out there and really battle the opposition. He won thirteen games while losing only four for us before retiring at the end of the season.

In a game against Cleveland, I was chasing a fly ball in deep right-center when I slammed into the auxiliary scoreboard at Yankee Stadium, breaking my arm in three places. Remembering when I had broken my collarbone while with the Cardinals back in 1941, I told Casey that my bones healed fast and that I could be ready to play in thirty days. With an arm out of commission, there wasn't much I could do for the Yankees, so I went back to the farm in Roxboro. I tied my healing arm to my side, and did what chores I could, like baling wheat and straw, for the next couple of weeks. I rejoined the club early to get the feel of swinging a bat again, and gradually increased my activity so that I was ready to play just four weeks after my collision with the scoreboard.

Still, my debut season in the American League didn't turn out to be very successful. I batted a meager .248 and played in only 69 games. Both of these numbers were career lows. The injury slowed me down some, and also, I was playing behind Hank Bauer, that Enos Slaughter fan from East St. Louis.

The Yankees ended up winning 103 games that year, more regular season victories than any team Casey ever managed. But that was the Cleveland Indians' year. Their centerfielder Larry Doby led the league in home runs and RBI's. Second baseman Bobby Avila was the batting champion. Two of the pitchers, Early Wynn and Bob Lemon, tied for the lead in victories. A third, Mike Garcia, had the lowest earned run average. And 35-year-old Bob Feller won 13 games and lost only three.

Of that impressive starting rotation, Lemon caused me the most trouble. He was a righthanded sinker-ball pitcher and, until the last year or so of his career, did a good job of keeping the ball down. Early Wynn, on the other hand, I didn't mind hitting against. He didn't like for hitters to swing through the middle on him, and he seemed to pitch up all the time. I also hit well against Feller and Garcia, but with three Hall-of-Famers (all having good years) and an ERA champion along with two top relievers (Don Mossi and Ray Narleski), the Tribe had one hell of a pitching staff. Cleveland won 111 games that year, eight more than we did. I never thought the Giants would beat them in the World Series. But they did, knocking off the Indians in four straight games. That just goes to show that you never know what can happen in baseball.

16

By early 1955, my marriage to Vickie wasn't working out at all. The differences were just too great. She was an entertainer from California; I was a country boy from North Carolina. There didn't seem to be too many things that we agreed on at this stage of our marriage.

The drive from Belleville to spring training turned out to be even worse than my trip home from Manila with the Ed Lopat All-Stars. We were having a few words as I drove down the highway at sixty miles per hour, when she suddenly opened her door and jumped out of the car.

I immediately hit the brakes as I saw her cartwheeling down the highway. Fortunately, a good samaritan stopped and we took her to the nearest hospital. She had a fractured skull, but miraculously, the injuries weren't life-threatening. After a week's stay in the hospital, I had half of my front seat taken out so that we could fit a mattress in the car. And that's how we travelled the rest of the way to spring training.

Like the Cardinals, the Yankees also trained in St. Petersburg. Their camp was named Miller Huggins Field, after the man who had managed the team from 1918 until his death in 1929. Training in the same town, I got a chance not only to see returning teammates, but also to visit with my former ones for the first time since I had been traded.

Vickie recovered quickly, but her father in California became ill, and she decided to spend time with him. When it was time to break camp, she flew west while the Yankees headed north. She would rejoin me later in the season, but by then, I believe we both realized that our marriage was on its last legs.

After my first ten games in the 1955 season, I was hitting only .111. At the end of April, the Yankees sold Johnny Sain and me to the Kansas City Athletics in exchange for Sonny Dixon, a big righthanded reliever who had been used in more games than any other American League pitcher the previous season.

The baseball writers were printing more obituaries of me as a player than ever, but in this case, it was Sain and Dixon who were nearing the end of the line. Johnny, who had been a top-notch reliever with the Yankees, had a harder time getting batters out with the A's, and this turned out to be his last major league season before a brilliant career as a pitching coach. Dixon was sent to the minors by the Yankees, and his major league days ended after only three games the following year. Another player who had just reached the end of the line was Phil Cavaretta. The White Sox first baseman hung up his spikes after appearing in only six games that April. He was the last player who had reached the major leagues before I had joined the Cardinals in 1938.

I was excited about going to Kansas City. In New York I'd been just another ballplayer, but Kansas City, which had just lured the Athletics from Philadelphia, was now the farthest west of all major league cities. The state of Missouri, and that region of the country, was where my fan base was. Also, I figured that I'd get more playing time with the Athletics than I would with the Yankees.

The news of the trade really had the adrenalin flowing in me. I cleaned out my locker and went back to the Concourse Hotel. There I packed my things, checked out and loaded up the car. Once again, I drove all night. Stopping only to purchase gasoline, I made it to my apartment in Belleville in 17 hours. I was still keyed up when I got there, so I bought a lawnmower and cut the grass. Then I caught a plane for Chicago and met my new teammates.

Lou Boudreau, a former shortstop, had just started as manager of the A's, but he already had 12 years of experience as a major league manager, and he really knew the game. He started me off as a pinch-hitter and utility outfielder, like Stengel had used me the previous season. I got 11 hits in my first 25 at-bats for Kansas

City and became the regular rightfielder against righthanded pitching.

Against southpaws, Boudreau used Bill Renna, another former Yankee. Renna was a big, powerful Santa Clara University alumnus who could hit the ball a long way if he ever got hold of it. He had been the Philadelphia A's regular rightfielder the year before, but strikeouts were a problem for him throughout his career.

My roommate Elmer Valo played center field. He had spent 13 years with the A's in Philadelphia, but the move to Kansas City seemed to agree with him. He also had gotten off to a great start with the bat. The two of us were constantly credited with being an inspiration to the rest of the club. He was platooned with Bill Wilson, who like Renna hit home runs, struck out a lot and had been an everyday player the year before.

Soon after I joined the club, Harry Simpson was purchased from the Indians. Harry hit over .300 and did a good job in the field.

Leftfielder Gus Zernial led the team in the power department with 30 home runs. Only Mantle, Berra and Larry Doby hit more American League home runs than the big, blond Texan did during the 1950's. Zernial got his nickname ("Ozark Ike") after a popular comic strip character of the day, while playing in the minor leagues.

We had a first baseman that year who could win games for us with his bat as well as his glove. Vic Power, a Puerto Rican, had been one of the first black players in the Yankees farm system. He had gone to the Athletics when the Yankees acquired Eddie Robinson before the 1954 season. It took him a year at Philadelphia to get adjusted to major league pitching, but when the team moved west, he was hitting the ball with authority. He was also about as smooth a first baseman defensively as I've ever seen. I told anyone who wanted to listen that Vic was the best first baseman in the league.

Second baseman Jim Finigan, like Power, had started as an Athletic's regular the year before when the team was in Philadelphia. Unlike Power, he hit well in Phillie, but his average dropped almost fifty points after the team moved.

Our shortstop Joe DeMaestri had played briefly with the White Sox and the Browns before joining the A's in '53. "Oats" was not a great hitter, but he did well enough defensively to hold the job for seven years before moving on to the Yankees as a utility infielder. Other than Power, Panamanian rookie Lopez was the best hitter in the infield.

Longtime Athletics catcher Joe Astroth was, by that time, near the end of his career. Sharing the duties with him was Billy Shantz, in his second and last year with the A's. At 6'1", Billy dwarfed his older brother Bobby, an outstanding pitcher, who was only 5'6", but Bobby had more of an impact on the game. I had faced Bobby before in All-Star games, but at this point, he was coming off arm trouble and wasn't as effective as he had been in Philadelphia. In fact, our whole pitching staff wasn't too hot that year. Our top winner, with twelve victories, was Art Ditmar. Vic Raschi had come over from the Cardinals and, like Sain, closed out a great career with a poor season.

Another former Cardinal ending his career with Kansas City that season was Cloyd Boyer. Cloyd was still giving it everything he had, but he was having a hard time getting anybody out. As Cloyd's playing days were coming to an end, his two brothers were just starting out. Clete was an 18-year-old bonus baby utility infielder on our team. He didn't get into many games that year, and would have been better off playing every day in the minors, but, at that time, there was a rule requiring bonus players to be on the major league squad. Meanwhile, brother Ken was making a great start to a solid career, replacing Ray Jablonski as the Cardinals' third baseman.

Lou Boudreau did a good job with the club. The year before in Philadelphia, the A's had won only 51 games and finished last. In 1955, we won 12 more games than the last Philadelphia club and ended up well ahead of the Baltimore Orioles and the Washington Senators. Our manager was nice enough to give me some of the credit for the improvement. Playing under Lou, I had a great year, hitting .322 for K.C., which gave me a .315 average for the season. That slowed down some of the whispers that my career was over.

I really enjoyed my playing days under Boudreau. He was a good guy and has always been a real gentleman. That's the reason I still play at his charity golf tournament every year.

While Lou and the coaches were wonderful to me out there, I just can't say enough about the Kansas City fans. The people in St. Louis had always been great to me, but I never had bigger ovations than those I received in Municipal Stadium.

The fans would cheer me whether I hit a home run or struck out. I'd get letters from people who lived in Missouri and other parts of the Midwest that said they used to go to Cardinals games, but since I had been traded, they were instead going to Kansas City. A fan club was started for me there, and even though I didn't stay with the A's very long, it lasted for about eight years. Each year, I still get Christmas cards from about 40 former members.

Those great fans voted me the Athletics' most popular player and presented me with a Chrysler Imperial on the last day of the season. We had finished 33 games behind the Yankees, but an overflow crowd turned out to see us off.

"We belong to you, to all of you in Kansas City," I told the cheering crowd, as I spoke for the organization. "I hope I have many more years in Kansas City."

That last remark brought out a yell from the stadium that could be heard in St. Louis.

Too bad I wasn't as popular at home. Vickie and I were getting along worse than ever, and we had separated in August. By the time I moved back to Belleville after the season, she had gone for good. The place looked like General Sherman had marched through. Everything in the apartment was torn apart. She had cut up all of my suits and shirts. The television was smashed. Holes were punched into the wall and burned into the carpet. Everything in the kitchen was demolished, including the gas stove.

Though my marriage was in tatters, I did have some luck during the off-season. Because of my popularity throughout the Midwest, the Joseph A. Schlitz Brewing Company hired me for promotional work. A's coach Harry Craft and Merle Harmon, now a football announcer but then the voice of the Kansas City A's, and I traveled together, covering nine states for the brewery. I'd go up around Des Moines, Iowa, and after making a couple of appearances in that area, I'd fly back to Kansas City, where I would get into my car and drive to Joplin, Missouri. Then I'd head out to Colorado, where I'd speak all over the state. We would appear in all kinds of places, even churches. I wouldn't mention the beer in my talks. Still, we must have helped the company. Schlitz became the country's leading brand of beer, even surpassing Anheuser-Busch's Budweiser.

17

After raising my batting average 57 points in 1955 over that of the previous season, I begged Parke Carroll, the Athletics general manager, to give me a raise. I'd never done well with general managers, and I didn't get a raise with him, either. Once again I had to sign for $20,000, which had been my salary since Breadon had cut me by $5,000 in 1951. That's what I made the rest of my years in the big leagues.

My salary may have been the same, but the Athletics were rapidly changing, and unfortunately, not for the better. Nowhere was this more apparent than in the outfield. Bill Wilson failed to make the team in spring training because of his inability to make contact. He was replaced by veteran outfielder Johnny Groth, who was picked up from Washington. My roommate Elmer Valo was traded after 13 seasons with the A's. In June, Bill Renna was used in a trade with the Yankees that landed us Eddie Robinson and rookie outfielder Lou Skisas.

Harry Simpson was the only outfield regular Boudreau used that year. Gus Zernial and I shared playing time with Groth and Skisas for the other two positions.

Simpson and Skisas hit well for us, and I batted about .280 for the Athletics in '56, but as a whole, the team played more like the late Philadelphia A's than a contender.

By August we were buried in last place, while the Yankees were in first. Casey and the boys had gotten off to a great start, but Mantle, Irv Noren and Norm Sieburn all came down with knee problems and the Yankees lost six games in a row at the beginning of the month. Weiss and Stengel were desperate for another left-handed-hitting outfielder.

After a game in Washington, I had plans to go out to dinner with my Schlitz coworker Harry Craft. I had just come out of the shower, when Lou Boudreau asked me to stop by his office after I got dressed. When I went in to see him, he asked me, "How would you like to go back to the Yankees?"

"I'm satisfied here in Kansas City," I replied. But, as it turned out, my opinion didn't make any difference.

"Well, we've sold you back to the Yankees," I was told.

So, instead of going out to dinner with Craft, I packed up my luggage and was escorted to the train station by Boudreau. I took a train to the airport and flew to New York, where all hell had broken loose in the Yankee clubhouse.

Because of the toll injuries had taken on the outfield, Casey had asked general manager George Weiss to bring me back. Weiss supposedly had not been too keen on the idea at first, pointing out that I was 40 years old, but Casey remained adamant about getting me. I heard the Yanks paid $50,000 for my contract, but I'm not sure. Making more news in New York than my re-acquisition was the name of the player they released to make room on their roster in order to pick me up. It was Phil Rizzuto.

The way I understand it, Casey and Weiss called in Rizzuto after they had reached their agreement with K.C. owner Arnold Johnson to buy me back. They asked the shortstop who they should let go in order to pick me up. Phil gave them several suggestions, but Weiss rejected all of them. That's how the 13-year Yankee veteran realized that he was finished as a player.

The news of the popular Rizzuto's release didn't please Phil's teammates at all, but there was nothing I could do about that. The decision was made by the Yankee organization, not by me. I liked Phil and had nothing against him at all. I had enjoyed him before as a teammate and was sorry to learn of his release. I also realized that he was three years younger than I, but Casey had made his mind up that he wanted an outfielder, and releasing Phil was the only move they thought possible at the time. Gil McDougald was doing a great job at short for the team that year, and there were other young infielders around like Billy Martin, Andy Carey and Bobby Richardson, who was my roommate for the rest of that season. Furthermore, Tony Kubek, viewed as the team's shortstop of the future, was just about ready to be promoted from the minor leagues.

Anyway, after I rejoined the club, we swept the Tigers in a double-header. I started both games in left field and went five-for-nine during the twin bill, with a home run, a triple and three singles.

From Yankee Stadium, we hit the road, going first to Chicago. We were tied in a game with the White Sox when I went to bat in the 12th inning against Dick Donovan. The righthander had held me hitless in my previous four trips that game, but this time I hit one out to beat him.

I really think I helped the Yankees win the pennant that year. Then came the World Series with my old arch rivals, the Dodgers. Before the Series started, Elston Howard came down with strep throat so bad that he had to be placed in the hospital. Since he was unavailable, Casey used me as the starting leftfielder.

We came up empty after the first two games at Ebbets Field, losing 6-1 and 13-8. But in the third, back at Yankee Stadium, the Dodgers had scored two runs off Whitey Ford, and led us by a run in the seventh. That inning, with two men on base, I hit a home run off fellow North Carolinian Roger Craig to win the ballgame for us.

The next day, we evened up the Series, and, in the fifth game, I had the honor of participating in Don Larsen's perfect game. I didn't even realize that Larsen had a perfect game going until about the eighth inning. When Don struck out Dale Mitchell to end the game, fans started streaming all over the field. I got off the field awful quick. Yankee Stadium was like a madhouse, with people running around and falling on the field and all. It's a wonder nobody got his hands spiked as players were trying to get the hell out of there.

We went back to Ebbets Field for game six. In the bottom of the tenth inning, Bob Turley and Clem Labine were locked in a scoreless tie when their second baseman Junior Gilliam led off for the Dodgers with a base hit. This brought Robinson to the plate. By this time, Jackie had been shifted to third base by Dodgers manager Walter Alston. After the Series, Jackie retired from base-ball. Standing out in left field, I didn't want to play too deep be-cause if Jackie were to hit a ground ball through the infield, I wanted to have a chance to keep Gilliam from getting to third with no outs. At the same time, I wanted to be able to go back if he hit a fly ball toward the fence. Jackie connected with Whitey's pitch and scorched a line drive to left-center. I broke for the fence and jumped for the ball, but I missed it as it hit off the wall. Gilliam scored on the play, giving the Dodgers a 1-0 victory.

On my way to the clubhouse after the defeat, I was met at third base by some reporter or other who said that I had misjudged the ball. Later, I found out that Billy Martin, watching the play from second base, had thought the same thing. In his autobiography, Martin said that he approached Stengel on the bus taking us back from Ebbets Field and told him, "If you play that National League bobo out there tomorrow, we're going to lose this thing."

I had hit .350 for the first six games in the Series, but by now Elston Howard was available. The catcher-outfielder had recov-ered from his throat condition, and it was he who played the sev-enth game for us. As it turns out, whoever played left field in that game was a mere formality, because we trounced the Dodgers 9-0 behind the pitching of Johnny Kucks. It was my third participation on a World Champion team.

Not too many years ago, Martin approached me and asked, "Do you know the reason that you didn't play in the seventh game of the 1956 World Series?"

I replied, "Yes, and you've been on my shit list ever since."

18

Being part of a World Championship team for the first time in ten years made me realize that I was lucky to have been able to play for two first-class organizations. I was heartbroken when the Cardinals traded me, but in each of the three seasons since I'd left, the team lost more games than it won. And, here I was in Yankee pinstripes playing in World Series games again.

Still, there were other things for me to think about after we beat the Dodgers in '56. In less than three years, I'd gone from the Cardinals to the Yankees to Kansas City and then back to the Yankees. The way baseball clubs had been shipping me from place to place made me realize that it was time to go back to my roots in order to make a home. Belleville had been great while I was playing in St. Louis, but the way things were going, I didn't know where I'd be from one year to the next.

I decided it was time to start getting ready for the rest of my life. I sold my interest in the jewelry store to my partner John Straub, and had a house built on the farm in North Carolina that I bought in 1939. I had always wanted to live there, and I felt the time was right to get on with my dreams. The house I built is still my home today, and I suppose it will be for the rest of my life.

I also was soon to embark on my fifth marriage, to Helen Spiker, a former airline stewardess I had met on a TWA charter flight. This marriage would last for 23 years, until our divorce in 1980. Helen and I would have three wonderful daughters, Gaye, Sharon and Rhonda. Helen was a good mother to our children, and added stability to the rest of my career and for some years afterward.

When I rejoined the Yankees in spring training, I was met by three of my former Kansas City teammates. Pitchers Bobby Shantz and Art Ditmar and third baseman Clete Boyer were picked up in a trade with the Athletics for outfielder Irv Noren, infielder Billy Hunter and pitchers Tom Morgan, Maurice McDermott, Rip Coleman and Jack Urban. As it turns out, the addition of Shantz and Ditmar was to more than make up for the departure of the four pitchers. Furthermore, my return to the club and the promotion of highly touted infielder-outfielder Tony Kubek made Noren and Hunter expendable.

I was being called by yet another nickname in 1957, "ol' 41," a nickname derived from my age. By that time I was the oldest player in the American League. Only one player in the majors was older. It was none other than Walker Cooper, the catcher I feel would have helped the Cardinals become a dynasty in the late '40s if only Sam Breadon hadn't sold him after the war. While Mort Cooper was nearing the end of his life (our '42 MVP died in Little Rock, Arkansas, on November 17, 1958, at the age of 45), little brother Walker was still playing baseball at the age of 42. And you'd never guess what team he was with in 1957. That's right— the St. Louis Cardinals. By then, however, he was primarily a pinch-hitter and didn't do much catching.

To this day, I'm best known for what I did as a Cardinal, but when the most famous photograph of me was taken, I was in a New York Yankees uniform—at least what was left of a New York Yankees uniform. I had just been thrown out of a ballgame for the only time in my career.

The picture was taken at Chicago's Comiskey Park that season on June 13. I wasn't even playing that day. Billy Pierce, the ace of the White Sox staff, was pitching against us, but I had always managed to hit that southpaw pretty good, so I was looking forward to getting into the game somehow.

The trouble started in the bottom of the first inning with one White Sox runner on base and none out. Art Ditmar was on the mound for us as Chicago's centerfielder, Larry Doby, came up to bat.

The Sox had a six game lead on us at the time, and tension was running high as Ditmar pitched two quick strikes to the powerful lefthander. Doby was a low ball hitter who crowded the plate as much as he could and didn't like balls going at his head. Ditmar was a fastball pitcher who disliked batters leaning toward the outside corner and didn't mind moving them back.

Ditmar fired a fastball high and inside. Doby was sent sprawling to the ground. The ball missed Doby and got by Elston Howard, who was stationed behind the plate.

As the runners advanced, Ditmar rushed to cover home. While he was there, he and Doby had a few words. That's all, words. Ditmar went back to the mound, and was ready to take the signals from Howard for the next pitch, when Billy Martin came in from second base to find out what the words were all about. When he found out, Martin had a few words of his own to yell at Doby. Whatever those words were, they were enough for Doby to drop his bat and head for the mound. Bill Skowron, the former Purdue halfback, charged the mound from first base, and downed the Sox outfielder with a flying tackle.

Both benches emptied as the players rushed toward the snowballing free-for-all. A bigger "Moose" than Skowron was next to join the brawl, as Chicago first baseman Walt Dropo threw his 6'6", 240-pound frame on top of it all. That's when I ran to the mound, where by then they were piled three deep. I grabbed Dropo by the collar and hollered for him to get up off Skowron. Then somebody jerked me back, but my hand held on to the big Sox first baseman's collar, causing him to choke a bit. That turned Dropo into a wild bull. He got up, grabbed me by the shirt and measured me for a right cross to the jaw.

That's when my roommate, Whitey Ford, came to my aid. Whitey jumped on Walt's back as the stampeding giant tried to get at me. He never did land any blows, but he ripped my uniform shirt to shreds. By the time the umpires and the Chicago police had calmed things down, my sleeves were still on, but the rest of the front of my uniform shirt was hanging down in front of me.

Doby, Dropo and I were kicked out of the game. As I was walking off the field, an umpire picked up my cap and put it on my head backwards.

Nobody was really hurt in this little mélee, but it ended up getting more attention than any other free-for-all I was ever in, including the one in 1940 between the Cardinals and the Dodgers when Medwick was beaned. That's because television had come into its own by 1957, and the people who were planning to watch baseball that afternoon got a good half-hour's entertainment thrown in extra. People still come up to me and say that was the greatest fight they ever saw on television. By the time the game continued, I was in the visiting team clubhouse, watching the game on television myself.

After the Yankees won that game, Will Harridge, then president of the American League, announced that Doby, Dropo, Ditmar, Martin and I had been fined $150 apiece for our parts in that fracas. Dan Topping was then quoted to say that he didn't feel that the fines for the Yankee players were justified and hinted that he would take care of them himself.

"If you pay the fines for them, it's going to cost you $5,000," Harridge reportedly warned the Yankees owner.

For me, this story didn't end until the following year when Casey quietly and discreetly handed me three fifty dollar bills. I don't know about the other guys. Ditmar was still with the club then, but we never asked each other about any money.

By that time, Martin was with the Detroit Tigers, his second club since leaving the Yankees. From then on, he bounced from club to club until he retired and became even more famous bouncing from club to club as a manager. His Yankee playing career ended two days after the brawl at Comiskey. Weiss sent him to Kansas City along with prospects Ralph Terry, Woodie Held and Bob Martyn for my A's teammate Harry Simpson and a young pitcher named Ryne Duren.

Billy was an aggressive player when he was with the Yankees and he was later a fine manager, but I think he could have been an even better one if he hadn't run his mouth so much. Maybe he mellowed a bit, but he got in too many fights over the years with players when he was out drinking with them in bars. I don't think you can have a player's respect if you do that. I think a manager is asking for trouble if he goes out drinking with his players. Casey had the right idea when he told his players to keep out of their hotel bars on the road because that's where he planned to do his own drinking. A manager doesn't have any business being around players in that kind of atmosphere.

Some people think that Martin was traded because of a barroom fight at the Copa Cabana about a month before the deal, when a few members of the team were celebrating the volatile second baseman's birthday and got into a shouting match with some other patrons in the club. I can't tell you anything about that because I wasn't there. For that matter, I never went to the Copa or any of the other places like that in New York. I did eat at Toots Shor's and another place that had great steak, Danny's Hideaway. But my favorite place to eat was called The Dutchman's, located at the Concourse Plaza, three blocks from Yankee Stadium. The owner really liked ballplayers. He always said guys in our profession had made him a success. When the likes of Babe Ruth and Shanty Hogan started frequenting his place, he was able to gain a sizeable clientele. It wasn't a fancy place. There was sawdust on the floor, but ballplayers sure got the royal treatment. Back then you could get the biggest steak in the house for only three or four bucks.

Martin's exit made Bobby Richardson the undisputed second baseman. He went on to do a great job there for the Yankees for many years to come.

Mantle was having another super year until the middle of August when he gashed his left leg. I was needed to play more the rest of the season. Kubek replaced him a lot in center field, and when Tony played center, I was usually the leftfielder.

With Mantle hurting, we lost ground to the White Sox until August 27, when we arrived in Chicago for a three game series. If the Sox had swept that series at Comiskey Park, they would have been only a half game behind us. Instead, we took all three games.

That third game led to my greatest moment with the Yankees, at least during the 1957 regular season. The time was ten minutes after four. I remember the time because it had been agreed before the game that we would not start an inning after four-thirty so that we could catch the train. The game was tied at one apiece and, coming to bat to start the eleventh, I knew that I was leading off the final inning before we left the ballpark for the train station. I swung at the first pitch, and, to the delight of all the gray uniforms that day, the ball flew deep into Comiskey's right field seats. It had to be one of the longest home runs I ever hit.

After cooling off the White Sox with that sweep in Chicago, we never looked back. We finished the season eight games ahead of Chicago with a record of 98 wins and 56 losses.

Our opponent in the World Series, the Milwaukee Braves, had won the National League by eight games. Coming in second were the Cardinals, with their highest finish in the standings since 1949. But, except for Stan Musial and Vinegar Bend Mizell, this was not my old team. By this time Frank Lane had taken over as general manager and had earned himself the nickname of "Trader", which he richly deserved. Lane made McKeon, who became known as "Trader Jack" while he was running the San Diego Padres, look gunshy. By 1957, just about all of my old Cardinal teammates were out of St. Louis. Musial would have been gone also, I understand, if Busch hadn't stopped yet another of Lane's trades.

Actually, three of my former Cardinal teammates were on the Braves team we faced in the World Series that year. Their second baseman was none other than Red Schoendienst, who really sparked the team after Milwaukee had picked him up from the Giants on the June 15 trading deadline that year. A year earlier, Lane had swapped him to New York for Alvin Dark. And earlier in the same month he traded Red, Lane sent backup catcher Del Rice to the Braves. Another Milwaukee substitute was Nippy Jones, who had accidentally ended my 1948 season with a batted ball.

I started the first game of the Series on the bench that day in Yankee Stadium while Kubek, the American League's Rookie of the Year that season, was in left field. In the sixth I entered the game, taking Mantle's spot in the lineup. In the bottom of the sixth, with Elston Howard on first base, I tagged my long-time

National League opponent Warren Spahn for a base hit. Carey followed with another single, and the Braves star lefthander then walked Yogi, scoring Howard for our third and last run of the day. It turned out to be one more than we needed, because Ford held the Braves to five hits and only one run, which was driven in by Schoendienst.

The next day, it was Andy Carey's turn to sit on the bench. Kubek played third and I was in left. In the bottom of the second with Milwaukee up 1-0, Lew Burdette walked me and Kubek singled me to third. Up to bat came Jerry Coleman, our player representative. Coleman was once the Yankees regular second baseman, but he was to retire as a player following the World Series and at this point in his career, he was basically a reserve. Anyway, he hit a ball that went a grand total of about 15 feet. Both Burdette and catcher Del Crandall scampered after the ball. Seeing that no one was covering home, I charged across the plate, tying the score.

I wish that had been my most important play, but it wasn't. In the top of the fourth, first baseman Joe Adcock got a base hit off Bobby Shantz, and rightfielder Andy Pafko singled him to second. Leftfielder Wes Covington lined a third consecutive base hit which scored Adcock. I threw the ball to third, but it got by Kubek and wound up in the Braves' dugout, enabling Pafko to score the second run on that play. Burdette held us scoreless the rest of the way. We had a good chance to catch up in the bottom of the sixth when I lined a shot that got by Covington in left field with Berra on first and only one out. I was able to leg out a double, but Yogi had to hold up at third and was unable to score as the next two batters rolled out.

It was not a pleasant trip as we headed cross country for the next three games. The Braves flew to Milwaukee; but when both your traveling secretary and your general manager hate airplanes, you take the train. There was something else that was not setting too well with me on that train ride: I knew I wasn't going to be in the starting lineup the next day against the right-handed Bob Buhl. Stengel, as it turns out, had been unhappy about the ball that I threw to Kubek in the previous game. It wasn't that my throw was bad. In fact, it was Kubek's error. Casey thought that I should have tried to nail Adcock at home on the play.

We were all glad for the long ride to finally come to an end, but when it did, things got even worse. It was decided that the team would stay 60 miles northwest of Milwaukee in a resort called Brown's Lake. The move was designed to give us some peace and quiet, but that quickly backfired when we found a crowd of people waiting for us at the train station.

We were in no mood to be pestered by a welcoming committee, and wasted no time heading to our rooms. Some of the fans got carried away and tried to get on the train. Casey was not impressed by these antics and was quoted as saying that they were "bush." That one quote followed us around like the plague during our entire stay in Wisconsin that year, and even the year after.

The Yankees did a pretty good job in the third game. Kubek's debut was totally unappreciated by his hometown fans, who greeted both of his home runs that day with a silence that was downright spooky. In the visitors' dugout and clubhouse, however, we showed our appreciation for the young man, who led us to a 12-3 victory.

The only thing the second game at County Stadium had in common with the first were the boos the fans shouted at Stengel every time he stuck his head out of the dugout. That didn't bother old Case. He blew kisses to the hostile people in the stands.

What did bother our manager, in that fifth game, was the outcome. The Braves took the lead in the fourth on Hank Aaron's home run. In the ninth, with a 4-1 lead, their starter Warren Spahn gave up a three-run homer to Elston Howard, which tied the game. In the top of the tenth, Hank Bauer tripled in Kubek to regain our lead, but it all ended in the bottom of that inning.

Nippy Jones led off the bottom of the tenth. Tommy Byrne threw a low one that got by Yogi Berra. Jones started running to first base like he'd been hit, but umpire Augie Donatelli ruled that the pitch was only a ball. As Jones and Donatelli argued, Connie Ryan, Milwaukee's third base coach, showed a smudge on the ball to the umpire: the ball had a shoe-polish stain. Donatelli then awarded Nippy first base, and it was the Yankees' turn to be unhappy. Felix Mantilla was sent in to run for Jones, and Casey replaced Byrne on the mound with Bob Grim.

After Schoendienst bunted Mantilla to second, it was time for me to enter the game. Once again, I was brought into left field, while Kubek moved to center replacing Mantle. I didn't have to wait long to get into the action. The next batter, Johnny Logan, drove the ball down the left field line, sending me to the wall. By the time I got the ball back into the infield, Logan was on second and the score was tied. The only other thing I did in that game was watch Eddie Matthews foul off a few of Grim's pitches before one sailed over the right field fence.

Even though I didn't get a chance to bat in the fourth game, I played regularly the rest of the Series. Mantle had strained a tendon in his left shoulder when Schoendienst fell on him as he was diving back into second base.

Schoendienst himself was finished for that World Series by the second inning of that last game in Milwaukee, when my former Cardinal teammate lunged at a ball that I had driven up the middle. I ended up with a base hit and he ended up with a pulled groin muscle on that play, his last of 1957.

Lew Burdette ended up shutting us out 1-0, but we were not without our chances to score in that game. After my base hit when Red got hurt, I took off for second on a hit-and-run. But Harry Simpson struck out and I was thrown out at second. In the fourth, McDougald hit what would have been a home run, but Wes Covington retrieved it with a miraculous catch. I then singled to left, but Simpson hit into a double play.

I guess Weiss didn't want to take any more flack from the press about the Yankees riding a train back to New York while the Braves flew. This time, we also chartered a plane.

Three Hall-of-Famers were now out of that series, but four others were still able to play, Hank Aaron and Eddie Matthews for the Braves and Yogi Berra and me for the Yankees. The sixth game was the 53rd Series game in Yogi's career. That put him one ahead of Phil Rizzuto for first on the all-time list. Others have since passed Rizzuto, but Yogi remains number one in this category.

Batting third for the Yankees, I was the first player to reach base in game six when I drew a walk off Bob Buhl in the bottom of the first. I walked again in the fourth and scored the game's first run as Yogi homered. "Bullet Bob" Turley, one of the game's fastest pitchers, performed brilliantly and we won the game 3-2.

For the final game, Casey sent Don Larsen to the mound. He also returned Mantle to centerfield and sent me to left, with Kubek at third.

Braves manager Fred Haney had planned to send Warren Spahn to the mound once again, but his star lefthander was bedridden with the flu. Haney then chose the crafty Lew Burdette, who had already won two games in the Series, including the shutout just three days before.

When Hank Bauer led off the bottom of the first against Burdette with a double, it looked like we were going to score off the hot pitcher that day. But things turned around when I followed with a ground ball back to Lou. Bauer was caught between second and third. As Hank scurried back and forth in his pickle, I hustled to second. That also backfired. Bauer somehow made it back to second base, and I was ruled out. I never got a hit that day and we never scored a run. Milwaukee scored four times in the fourth and again in the eighth. The Braves won easily.

It was the first and the last time I played for a team that lost the World Series.

19

Another year, another nickname. After my birthday on April 27, I started being known as "Old 42." By then, I was the oldest player in baseball. (The Cardinals had released Walker Cooper during the previous World Series.)

With Hank Bauer, Mickey Mantle, Norm Siebern, Harry Simpson and either Yogi Berra or Elston Howard available for outfield duty, I found myself being used as a pinch-hitter more than ever. Casey would tell the writers that I was the only guy on the Yankees who could go up there to bat with the team eight runs down and get on base for him to start a rally.

Casey would have a player pinch-hit for somebody in the first inning if we had a rally going and he thought that a guy on the bench could get us some more runs. A lot of the players didn't like it, but you couldn't argue with the way the team kept winning ballgames. Once, before I joined the Yankees, Gil McDougald was having a great game at the plate against the Tigers. He had gone four for four, but then Casey sent up John Mize to bat in his place. Mize hit a home run, so what can you say?

In 1958, I came up to pinch-hit 48 times, more than anyone else in the league. I still wanted to play regularly, but I had adjusted to being a pinch-hitter. In order to stay in the game, a player can adjust to anything if he's got the heart and soul to do it. Pinch-hitting is not an easy job, but I made myself do the best I could. In time, I got to the point where I enjoyed it.

I could almost tell in which situations Casey was going to use me. I would then go down to the side of the dugout and stretch my legs to loosen up. That way, if he called on me, I was ready to hit.

Contrary to what some people have said and written about me, I did not sit next to Casey on the bench; he would sit on the upper end. Frank Crosetti, the third base coach, was always next to our manager, while I sat with most of the players down at the other end.

The last two years I was with the Yankees, Ryne Duren was the best reliever in baseball. By 1958, the powerful righthander was 29 years old and in his third organization, but had appeared in only fifteen big league games. As a pitcher, his blazing speed was offset by problems finding the plate. Off the field, his reputation suffered because of trouble with the bottle. He didn't overcome his drinking problem until after he was through with baseball, but the Yankees helped him with his control soon after they picked him up as a throw-in in the Billy Martin deal. It turned out that his eyesight wasn't too good, and some nice thick glasses turned him into a great minor league pitcher.

Once he was promoted to the Yankees, he was something fearsome to behold for a team starting a late inning rally against us. Casey would bring in Duren and the first warmup pitch would be fired to the screen. When the poor hitter saw those wild warmup pitches, those thick horned-rim glasses, and the shadows gathering around the plate, he'd get a little shaky because everyone could see that Ryne could really throw that ball hard.

Speaking of good pitchers, on September 20, Hoyt Wilhelm, then pitching for the Baltimore Orioles, had the finest day in his Hall-of-Fame career. The knuckleballer was fooling all of the mighty hitters in the great Yankee lineup that day.

It was overcast, and a drizzling rain came and went. But Hoyt Wilhelm was consistent that day. Only Richardson and Coleman reached base, and they did it on walks. Our pitching wasn't bad. Larsen threw six scoreless innings, and Shantz did a good job in the seventh and eighth except for a home run by Baltimore's catcher, Gus Triandos.

With Bauer in right field and Siebern in left, I watched most of that game from the bench. But as the ninth inning approached, knowing that our pitcher was due up, I figured it was just about time for me to go to work. I grabbed myself a bat and started limbering up with it in the runway behind the visitor's dugout at Memorial Stadium. Sure enough, with one out in the top of the ninth, Casey called on me to pinch hit for Shantz.

Normally, as I mentioned earlier, I took the first pitch when I was up to bat. But going up against a knuckleball pitcher is a different story. With guys like Wilhelm or Dutch Leonard, whom I had faced in the National League, I always went up there with the intention of trying to hit the first pitch. That's because, if a knuckleballer gets two strikes on you, he can throw the ball just a little bit differently and catch you off guard. Wilhelm had already struck out eight Yankees that day, and I didn't want to be number nine.

I swung at Wilhelm's first offering. Fortunately for me, I connected and sent a line drive to right center. Fortunately for Hoyt, rightfielder Willie Tasbey made a great leaping catch. Bauer then popped out, and Wilhelm had his no-hitter.

The Yankees were a dominant team in 1958. We won 25 of our first 31 games and never looked back. We finished with 92 victories, ten ahead of the second place White Sox. Mantle led the league in home runs. The left fielders, Norm Siebern, Elston Howard and I, all hit over .300. Whitey Ford led the league in ERA, and Bob Turley, who won the Cy Young Award, led the AL in victories with a 21-7 record.

With Siebern winning a gold glove in left field and Howard hitting so well at that position, I thought I might be used some in right field during the upcoming Series because Hank Bauer's wrist had been bothering him.

The Milwaukee Braves had also repeated as pennant winners, beating the second place Pittsburgh Pirates by eight games. As we headed to County Stadium to begin the Series, Stengel approached Bauer.

"Your wrist is going to keep you from playing, ain't it?" asked our manager.

"There ain't nothing wrong with my wrist," insisted Bauer. "I can play, and don't you dare try to stop me."

"Okay," replied Casey. "You play."

And I sat. I was on the bench the entire first game to watch us lose in ten innings when centerfielder Bill Bruton, who had missed the entire 1957 Series with a bad knee, drove a Ryne Duren pitch to the wall between Mantle and Bauer, scoring Joe Adcock.

Lou Burdette kept his whammy on the Yankees for a fourth consecutive game the following day as the Braves pounded Bob Turley and Duke Maas and defeated us 13-5. I pinch-hit for Andy Carey in the eighth inning, but grounded out.

Back at Yankee Stadium, Don Larsen was pitching the second-best World Series game of his career when I went to bat for him in the seventh. I drew a walk and Bauer followed with a home run. He had previously driven in the only other two runs scored in that game with a single in the fifth. We won 4-0. The next day, the Braves came within one game of repeating as champions when Spahn shut us out. He struck me out in the eighth as I was pinch-hitting for Kubek. Braves, 3-0.

In the final game at Yankee Stadium, we finally got to Lew Burdette, scoring six runs in the seventh. Bob Turley had regained his form and shut out the Braves, 7-0, on five hits.

My final World Series appearance was in Game 6, after we had returned to Milwaukee to decide the championship once and for all. Batting for Kubek in the sixth with the score tied and men on first and second, I moved the runners up on an infield grounder. They didn't score, but we eventually won that game 4-3 in the tenth off Gil McDougald's homer.

I was not involved in the final game, but my friend Bill Skowron sure was. He drove in two runs off Burdette with a single and a homer, giving us a 3-2 victory and the Series.

In addition to regaining the World Championship, the Yankees picked up some individual records. Yogi Berra was now the all-time leader in World Series hits. Hank Bauer extended his record post-season hitting streak to 17 games, before he had gone hitless in the fifth game. And Enos Slaughter became the oldest player ever to appear in a World Series.

20

The Yankees got off to a terrible start in 1959. On May 20, we lost to the Detroit Tigers. Frank Lary, their righthander, seemed to have a whammy on the Yankees, the same way Max Lanier did against the Dodgers when he pitched for the Cardinals in the forties. That loss dropped the Yankees into last place for the first time in almost twenty years; Mickey Mantle was booed even as he circled the bases after hitting a home run.

Needless to say, if Mantle was booed in his home park when he hit a home run, he was also booed when he did something less. The frustrated fans were really taking it out on him. After hitting .300 or better for five years and leading the league in homers for three of four years, Mantle saw his average way down, as well as his power production. Most importantly, after helping the Yankees to pennants for seven of the past eight years, his team was in last place.

It was sad for me to watch the way the fans were making Mickey the scapegoat for the team's terrible start. A lot of people thought he was deadbeating when he would walk instead of run to his position in center field. He would start from the dugout jogging and walk the rest of the way. I was 43 years old that year and I did what I always did going to the outfield—I ran out there at full speed. I wasn't trying to show him up. I had been doing it ever since he was four years old, and I still do it today during old-timer's games. But some of the fans thought that their 27-year-old superstar from Commerce, Oklahoma, was dragging, and they really gave him hell for it. I don't think they realized how bad his legs were hurting him. He had to have bandages put around his knees all the years I was with him on the Yankees. Those legs of his were so bad that I remember seeing opposing pitchers actually back off from the rubber and wait until he could get into position in the batter's box.

Mickey was even worse on himself. Striking out was really bad on his ego. Unfortunately, he struck out 126 times in 1959, more than anyone else in the majors. That was his worst year for striking out, and that's saying a lot, considering that he eventually set all-time records in that unflattering department. With the strikeouts came the boos and the frustration. I think Mantle got down on himself even more than the fans did. He was fighting with himself and I think that this hurt him as a ballplayer.

I think he could probably hit a ball as far as anybody I've ever seen. You can talk about Reggie Jackson or anyone else, but I think Mickey was as strong a player as ever swung a bat. And with all that power, he also had blazing speed. What a talented player he was! In my estimation, he could have been just about the greatest ballplayer who ever lived, if he just had not been so hard on himself.

The greatest player I ever saw was my own longtime teammate Stan Musial. I think Ted Williams was probably the greatest hitter I've ever seen, but between Ted and Musial, I'd have to take Stan as an all-around player over Williams.

Mantle was a great defensive centerfielder. Even with bad legs, he had enough speed to make some great catches in left-center or right-center. Despite Mantle's speed, I still have to say that Terry Moore was, in my mind, the greatest defensive centerfielder I ever played alongside.

Speaking of great defensive players, Clete Boyer joined the Yankees that year. He had been a teammate of mine at Kansas City and would go on to become a fine-fielding third baseman for the Yankees. He was still having trouble hitting the breaking ball and the changeup, but he eventually improved. He had power, but I think his glove kept him in the big leagues a lot more than his bat did.

As the season wore on, the Yankees started moving up in the standings, but it became clear by the end of August that we would wind up the season behind the White Sox and the Indians. In September, we were playing Washington when I went to bat against a big righthander named Russ Kemmerer. He threw me a sinker ball and I foul-tipped it to the top of my left foot. I'll tell you, that damned foot felt like it had been struck by a cannonball. I got down on one knee and found, to my dismay, that I couldn't get back up, the pain was so sharp. Finally, I had to leave the ballgame.

When the club left for Baltimore, I stayed in New York and took treatments for my injury. I ended up missing two weeks. When I rejoined the club, I still couldn't run, but I was available to pinch-hit. One day, Casey approached me and said, "We're going to finish third, but you might get a chance to play in another World Series this year."

"Milwaukee needs a lefthanded hitter," the old Professor continued. "I know it's after the first of September, but if they win, they might be able to get permission to keep you on their World Series roster."

He was also talking about a chance to battle head-to-head again against my long-time archrivals, the Dodgers. They were the Los Angeles Dodgers by then, and they were in a tight pennant race against the Braves.

The chance to play in my fourth World Series in four years sounded great, but I felt that I should be up front about my physical problems.

"Casey, you know I can't run," I reminded him.

"Well, go ahead and talk to Mr. Weiss," he answered.

So I hobbled in to Mr. Weiss's office, and we talked for a while about my foot problems. Finally, he called John McHale in Milwaukee and put me on the phone with the Braves general manager.

"John, I can't run," I told him.

"Can you pinch-hit?" he asked.

"Yes, that I can do," I answered.

"Well, if you can pinch-hit, you might be able to help us," replied McHale, pointing out: "We've got to beat some tough righthanders on our trip to the West Coast if we're going to win the pennant. Don Drysdale for the Dodgers and Sad Sam Jones for the Giants are giving everybody in the league trouble this year."

The challenge was too much to pass up. After being sold to the Braves, I was back in the National League for the first time in over five years. Too bad I couldn't have left that pain in my left foot in New York; it came along with me as I joined Milwaukee the next day.

My new manager was Fred Haney, who had managed the St. Louis Browns during my early days with the Cardinals. In my first game under him, he sent me up to pinch-hit against Bob Purkey of Cincinnati. I connected for a base hit off the Reds' lanky righthander and was promptly removed for a pinch-runner.

After we flew to Los Angeles, Haney didn't ask me if I could play, he just put me in left field against Drysdale and the Dodgers at their new home, the Coliseum. I hobbled around in the outfield, but got a base hit off the Dodger ace to beat them 2-1. The Dodgers, though, came back to beat us the next day.

From there, we flew up to San Francisco to take on the Giants in *their* new home. I got a base hit against Sad Sam Jones to tie the score, and Del Crandall, who was by this time the National League's best catcher, singled to drive me in with the winning run.

That was my last hurrah as a major league ballplayer. The Giants beat us the next day, and we flew on to Philadelphia. There, the ground was so hard at Connie Mack Stadium that I could hardly walk. Regretfully, I approached my new manager.

"My foot is hurting so bad that I just can't play on this ground," I told him.

I didn't realize it at the time, but with those words, I was done as a major league ballplayer. I watched helplessly on the sidelines as the Braves fought the Dodgers to a tie at the end of the regular National League season. For the third time, a team I played for tied for the pennant.

We lost the first playoff game at County Stadium as the Dodgers catcher, John Roseboro, hit a home run in the seventh inning to beat us. After the game, they got on their plane and we got on ours, and we all headed for Los Angeles.

In Game 2, we had a four run lead going into the bottom of the ninth during what turned out to be the last game in which I was officially part of a major league team. Fred Haney used all of his available pitchers except Bob Buhl, who had pitched the day before, but the Dodgers scored five runs to beat us.

Having played in two World Series against these guys as well as being teammates with them for a brief period, I can say that the Milwaukee Braves of the late fifties were tremendously talented.

With rightfielder Hank Aaron, Pitcher Warren Spahn and third baseman Eddie Matthews, they were obviously a great team, but McHale, Haney and the Milwaukee fans had more going for them than the contributions of those three Hall-of-Famers. I played alongside another excellent centerfielder named Bill Bruton. He wasn't a Terry Moore out there, but then nobody was, as far as I was concerned.

Another fine outfielder on that club was Andy Pafko. He was a handy guy to have around because he could play several different positions. He was 36 years old then. Like me, he had spent most of his career with the same club, the Chicago Cubs. I always thought a lot of Pafko, and we're still good friends today. I see a lot of him at baseball functions. Another guy who really helped out was shortstop Johnny Logan. When the chips were down, he often came through with clutch base hits. He was a fiery little guy, good for morale, just talking all the time.

It was a fine group of teammates I had and, even though I hadn't been with Milwaukee for long, I really felt bad for them when they just missed out on a third straight World Series.

The guys on the Braves were nice enough to vote me a $300 award from their share of second place money that year, for the three weeks I had spent with them. Meanwhile, the Yankees didn't cut me in for one penny of their share of third place money. I guess my comment about some of them thinking that Casey was in his second childhood must have gotten under some skins. But I couldn't help it. I've always been the type to say what I feel, and let the chips fall where they may.

I had to be disappointed with my low batting average and the Yankees poor showing that year, as well as the heartbreaking end of the Braves season. But I was bothered most by that damn left foot of mine. I was getting tired of the pain shooting up my leg every time I stepped on it. Finally, I had a podiatrist in Roxboro check it out. Dr. Coonan took X-rays and informed me that the third metatarsal on that foot was broken. He devised a steel plate for my shoe, to wear throughout the winter. Since I was playing for New York at the time of the injury, I sent Dr. Coonan's bill to George Weiss. The Yankee general manager asked to see copies of the X-rays, which I sent him.

Weiss was not without his detractors. Like Branch Rickey and Sam Breadon, he has been criticized by many for being tight with a nickel. But his response to my reimbursement request really warmed my heart. First of all, he paid the doctor bill. Also, he enclosed a letter thanking me for the help I had given his ballclub during the years I spent with the Yankees. The letter went on to say that he had found out that the Yankees had not voted me a share of the team's third place money. There was another check in that letter, this one for $929. A full share for Yankee players that year was $1,229. Weiss had taken that amount, subtracted the $300 I had gotten from the Braves, and paid me the difference. That's what I remember the most about George Weiss. I still have that letter today.

21

I started off 1960 in hopes of catching on with a major league club as a pinch-hitter and utility outfielder, but nobody seemed interested in my services. I believe that an American League team would have picked me up if they had the designated-hitter rule, but that didn't go into effect until 1973. If I could have landed myself a spot on a big league roster in 1960, I would have been one of the few ballplayers to play in four different decades.

Let me make this very clear: I wasn't at all upset with the Braves for not keeping me on their roster over the winter. I couldn't blame them for not hanging on to a 44-year-old guy like me when they had some young prospects that they didn't want to lose in the draft. But nobody can convince me there wasn't a major league club in 1960 I could have helped out, at least as a reserve.

Still, though, I can say that I played professional baseball in four different decades. After I was unable to find a job at the winter meetings in Louisville, I got a call from my old teammate and manager Marty Marion. By then, he was part owner of the American Association franchise at Houston. At the time, Houston was the Chicago Cubs' top farm team, but Marion and his partner, Milt Fishman, were hoping to be awarded a major league expansion franchise for that Texas city. As it turned out, they didn't get it, but that's not what Slats was calling me about. He wanted to know if I'd be interested in becoming a player-manager with his triple-A team. I told him that I really was hoping for a chance to play another year in the big leagues, but, if I couldn't, I sure wanted to stay in baseball in some capacity.

I asked for some time to make up my mind, and he gave me a week. When he called me up seven days later, I became his new player-manager.

Less than an hour after I accepted the job, I got another phone call, this one from New York. I was offered the job of color commentator for the Baltimore Orioles. But I had already given Marty my word, and I wasn't going to go back on it.

For years the Houston Buffaloes had been a Texas League farm club of the Cardinals. The year I had the club in the American Association, the nickname had been shortened to Buffs. We played at Buff's Stadium and believe me, it was nothing like the air-conditioned Astrodome where the Houston ballclub plays today. The heat didn't really bother me. Baseball is a game for hot weather anyway. But those damn mosquitoes that swarmed our ballpark were something else. Some of those pests were so big that you could have put saddles on them. In the dugout, we always had five-gallon containers of repellant attached to long-nozzled pumps. We constantly sprayed that repellant on ourselves to the point that we actually soaked our uniforms in it. Still, it was better than being eaten alive by those flying vampires.

I was fortunate to have some great ballplayers at Houston. Outfielder Billy Williams and third baseman Ron Santo both went on to star for the Cubs for many years. Dick Ellsworth and Jim Brewer both ended up with respectable major league pitching careers. We had a tall righthander named Joe Schaffernoth, who was promoted to Chicago at midseason and got a lot of work in the Cubs bullpen for the next couple of years.

Santo was also promoted at midseason. He was only twenty years old, and when I joined the team, Marion was planning to send him back down to double-A ball at San Antonio. But, I wanted to keep him, and he did a great job for me. He was a good-fielding third baseman who could hit with power. I didn't realize at the time that he was a diabetic who had to take insulin shots each day.

Billy Williams was a quiet young man who often got homesick. Whenever he took off for his home in Whistler, Alabama, I'd have to replace him, but he had a good season and went on to be National League Rookie of the Year in 1961. After all those great years he ended up having for the Cubs, I was glad to see the writers finally vote him into the Hall of Fame. And talk about power, he can still zip those balls out of the park in Old Timer's games like he did in his prime.

Managing these kids made me think more about the early part of my baseball career than I had in years. I tried to remember how my old minor league managers handled me. And wouldn't you know it, Eddie Dyer was in town at the time. He was out of baseball and operating an insurance agency. I got to see him quite often that year.

Houston, in those days, seemed to be a Mecca for old Cardinals. Dyer had his old pitching ace Howie Pollet working at his insurance agency. So was Jeff Cross, a utility infielder for us for a couple of years after the war. Marion, who Cross had backed up, was of course involved in the local baseball scene, and Joe Medwick had preceded me as a player-manager for the Houston club.

Once again, I had my share of physical problems in 1960. I had worn a steel plate in my shoe throughout the previous winter to get my foot back in shape, but I had to undergo surgery for an unrelated reason after pinch-hitting during a game in Minneapolis and legging out a triple. As I was standing on third base, I suddenly went blind. My eyes just went blank. I shook my head a few times, and my vision came back, so I stayed in the game. The next night, as I pinch-hit and was thrown out at first, the same damned thing happened, so I was sent back to Houston and examined by a specialist named Fred Guilford. Dr. Guilford discovered that I had somehow punctured an eardrum, and my temporary attacks of blindness were actually being caused by my inner ear problems.

That meant it was time for me to go under the knife again. During the operation, Dr. Guilford cleaned everything up, and put a new lining in my ear. He grafted eighteen pieces of skin off my arm to make the lining, but it turned out to be the greatest thing that could have happened to my hearing. I went from being 65% deaf in that ear (the result of tonsillitis in my childhood) to hearing 17% above normal after surgery. Now, that's good in some ways and a problem in other ways. To this day, when I fly in an airplane, the engine seems so loud that when I land, my ear is still buzzing. And that makes it hard for me to understand what people are saying for the next hour or two.

The operation caused me to miss some playing time. I was in the hospital for four or five days, but I was back managing within a week.

Houston finished third in the regular season standings for the American Association that year, but we almost captured the league championship. Denver finally beat us in the seventh game of the playoffs.

For some reason that I don't know to this day, the Cubs didn't renew my contract. So I ended the year the way I started it, looking for a job.

22

Marty Marion may have helped extend my career in pro baseball beyond the fifties, but it was a man named Herb Brett who pushed hard for me to get the last job I ever had in the business. He had been a pitcher at Danville in 1935, and he ended up running that club for some years. By 1961, he was still a minor league general manager, except he had moved to Raleigh. As owner of the Raleigh Caps in the Carolina League, Brett had just switched his team's major league affiliation to the New York Mets. Actually, the Mets did not have a major league team in '61, but the organization had just been awarded a National League expansion franchise. It's hard to imagine New York as an expansion team city, but you have to realize that the Giants and the Dodgers had recently left town, and lots of fans and influential people from there had been screaming for another franchise.

The new organization had not yet hired a manager for its Carolina League club, and Brett really wanted me to be his player-manager once he found out I was available. I was interested in the position because it gave me a chance not only to stay in baseball, but also to live on the farm, because the ballpark was only about an hour's drive from my house.

Finally, Herb talked Charlie Hurt, who was acting as the organization's general manager, into letting me have the player-manager position.

Spring training that year was in Mobile, Alabama. Along with the coaches and the scouts, there seemed to be hundreds and hundreds of kids, but unfortunately, not a whole lot of talent.

Once I looked over the Raleigh roster, I knew that the kids I had would be severely overmatched in the Carolina League. The scouts didn't want to admit this fact because they had signed the players. One scout even said to me, "Why, you've got at least fifteen $75,000 ballplayers on your team."

"If I do, then the woods are full of them," I replied. Seventy-five thousand dollars was exactly three times more than I had ever made as a major leaguer.

I remember telling Charlie Hurt on the telephone, "I haven't got a ballplayer that could play in Class D ball, much less Class B."

"Do the best you can with them and we'll take care of you," he assured me.

They took care of me, all right. It was like our clubhouse had a revolving door. They ran 54 youngsters through the team that year. Predictably, we finished on the bottom, and I got fired.

Herb Brett and I had absolutely no say in the personnel moves on the team. All of that was handled out of New York. Brett and I wanted to sign Jim Roland, a lefthander who had been striking out eighteen batters a game playing high school ball in Raleigh, but the organization wouldn't let us do it. We had a pitcher on our team named Tracy Rivers who threw a no-hit, no-run game for us—and they released him the next day.

Managing a last place team wasn't much fun, but at least I was able to go out on a better note as a player. For the first time since my last World Championship year with the Yankees, I was able to play without any serious injuries or illnesses. As a utility out-fielder, I had a good year for the Caps. It seemed like every time we played in Durham, I would get a base hit to right field.

Following the season, I paid my way to the Louisville winter meetings hoping to land another job in baseball. But this time, there were no takers.

I still think I could have helped a club as a utility outfielder, but I was almost 45 years old and didn't give much thought to returning to the major leagues as a player. American players weren't going to Japan at the time, but I really wanted to remain in baseball in some capacity. I was willing to be a major or minor league coach or perhaps a scout, anything for a chance to stay with the game that I loved. I contacted practically all the major league clubs and kept getting the same response: "Nothing available."

The "nothing available" that hurt the most came from the St. Louis Cardinals. I had sweat my blood and guts for that organization from 1935 until 1954, but they never offered me a job of any kind. Bing Devine, the general manager at that time, wouldn't even talk to me about a job. All these years, many Cardinal scouts have told me that they tell their prospects to strive to play like Enos Slaughter. I'm curious if those prospects ever wondered why there was nothing available for Enos Slaughter in the Cardinals organization after he was through as a player.

Maybe the reason I couldn't get a job was that I always spoke my piece if I had something to say. I might have ruffled some feathers in the Mets organization by giving them my frank evaluation of the talent on the club. But lying about it wouldn't have won any more ballgames or helped the young players. To this day, I don't believe you're doing anybody a favor just by saying what he wants to hear. You've got to tell him the truth, or what you believe to be the truth.

Finally, I decided that if I had to kiss somebody's rear end to stay in baseball, then it was time to get out.

23

After 1961, I stayed home and returned to the only trade I knew before I could play baseball. And I've been farming ever since.

My oldest brother Daniel had been operating the farm for me. When I couldn't get back into baseball, at first he and I worked on the farm together. After his wife died, he moved to my farm and lived by himself in a house near me for the next eight years.

In 1970 I got a call from Eddie Cameron, then athletic director at Duke University. He offered me a part-time job, that of baseball coach. It didn't take me long to decide to take him up on his offer. Duke is only 30 miles from my home; I could stay on the farm, just like I did when I managed for the Mets in Raleigh.

I still had plenty of time for farming, because my new job called for me to work for only four months of the year. My first month was at the beginning of the academic year, September. Then, in the spring semester, I was to coach the team in February, March, and April. I followed that schedule for the next seven years.

I enjoyed the time I spent at Duke very much, even though it wasn't easy to win ballgames. The school's athletic department didn't give scholarships for baseball. That fact made competing in the Atlantic Coast Conference rough. North Carolina, North Carolina State, Clemson and Maryland had strong baseball programs with full scholarships.

We did have one advantage over the other ACC schools. None of them allowed their football players to play baseball, but Duke's football coach Mike McGhee would let me use his players in conference games. Too bad I couldn't use them for non-conference games. Teams like East Carolina from the Southern Conference and High Point from the Carolinas Conference had great ballclubs while I was coaching at Duke.

The football players were not able to practice as much on baseball as they needed to. A lot of them would show up for baseball practice wearing their football pants. They would throw a little bit and swing the bat a few times, but they couldn't work out or do too much of anything else.

Speaking of bats: I was coaching when the conference changed from wooden bats over to aluminum. We had been breaking bats right and left, and with the tiny budget I was on, it was bankrupting the program. I liked the idea of aluminum bats because we needed the money to be spread around for other things. I've heard some talk about the possibility of professional baseball switching to aluminum bats. Now, that's not a good idea. The way some of those guys can hit the ball, it could take a pitcher's head off.

Finally, in 1977, Duke let me go. They claim that they never fire anybody, but they sure fired me. Still, I don't take anything away from the school because my contract wasn't renewed. To me, Duke University has been my second love, right behind baseball. I show my Blue Devil loyalty in an unusual way. Since I had my last divorce in 1980, I've cooked all my meals for myself. (It helps that I have a microwave oven, but I'm not a bad cook all the same). Anyway, sometimes I bake pies to give the girls on the Duke women's basketball team. I have season's tickets for the men's basketball games, too. I've pulled for Duke all of my life, and probably always will.

My last coaching experience came when Piedmont Technical College was founded in my hometown of Roxboro. The school wanted to start a baseball program, so they asked me if I would be interested in helping them out. At Piedmont Tech, we didn't even have a field to play on. We had to take our infield practice at the local high school field. There wasn't an overabundance of talent on the team, but we had a lot of fun anyway.

Since coaching at Piedmont Tech, I've been a full-time farmer. I raise a little tobacco, and piddle a little here and there.

After living on my farm for eight years, Daniel remarried and moved to Stem, North Carolina, just below Oxford. Until he remarried, Daniel still helped around the farm. After marriage he and his wife Elva fished, and just enjoyed their retirement years.

With Daniel living in Stem with Elva, I took over all the farming chores on my land myself. Farming is the life for me. I was born and raised on a farm, and I hope to stay on the farm for the rest of my life.

I love the open country. It's so peaceful and quiet here. I enjoy being able to get up in the morning and breathe this fresh air. We don't have any real pollution. I feel that people who live in the country are just healthier than people who live in the city.

Of course, farmers are not without their problems. Look at Gaylord Perry. He made a lot more money than I did playing in the major leagues, but he had to declare bankruptcy soon after he stopped playing ball. His farm just ate up all his hard-earned cash.

This is a great country we live in, but it sure wouldn't last very long without farmers. They raise what we eat. The crops, the cattle, the chickens, the hogs. People keep telling me about the government doing this and doing that, but I don't think the government is standing up for the farmers the way it should.

Congress and the Department of Agriculture came along with the Farm Home Administration a few years ago. They encouraged a lot of young people to go into farming in a big way. So these people borrowed money for heavy equipment and other things they needed to get started. Things didn't turn out at all well for a lot of these folks. I know of one boy, for instance, who paid back the administration over $115,000, and they turned around and cut him off. He lost everything he had. They had said they were going to "take care" of him. And they did—but not the way they had promised.

Today there are so many young farmers going under like that. I know of another boy who would rather farm than eat. But there's no way he can keep going if he continues to lose money every year. It's come to the point where you don't see too many young farmers. They just can't see a light at the end of the tunnel.

If the government says it is going to do things, then why aren't they done? Billions of dollars are being given away by the United States to foreign countries. Hell, people are starving right here in this country. I don't mind helping other people, but I still think folks at home should be taken care of first.

Now, you understand this is a tobacco farmer talking, but as long as I'm griping about the government, let me have a few words about its many campaigns to get people to stop smoking. They do what they can to keep people from buying cigarettes, and to those that do, they tell them, "You can't do this" and "You can't do that." This is supposed to be a free country, but the government keeps driving this stuff down your throat. But you don't hear these politicians say anything at all about booze and liquor. That must be because half of the politicians sit around and drink all the time. People are dying from alcoholism and cirrhosis of the liver, too, you know. Furthermore, I can't help but wonder if people realize what kinds of insecticides are sprayed on the vegetables they eat. If it kills bugs and bacteria, what's going to keep it from hurting you?

As for me, I never smoked. I've chewed tobacco, however, since I left the service. Still do. I especially enjoyed chewing tobacco when I was playing baseball, but I think I appreciate it even more today. I feel that if I get on a tractor or go hunting or fishing and have myself a good, tasty chew of tobacco in my mouth, it just relaxes me all over.

As I've said earlier in this book, I can relax better and I just feel better when I'm active. I still do most of the work on the farm myself. I very seldom hire any help until I get ready to harvest my tobacco. Actually, I work with my brother-in-law John Walker. I help him plant his crop and he helps me plant mine. We each hire labor during the harvest season. Then each of us bags up his own crop. We usually take our tobacco to market together.

I can't go on enough about how I enjoy working on the farm. I was disappointed about not being able to stay in baseball and, later, even more disappointed about not being voted by the writers into the Hall of Fame, but I've always been able to get out in that field on my tractor and, for the time being, forget about my problems.

In 1970, I had a chance to get back into professional baseball again, but this turned out to be one of my more bizarre experiences in the game, in a new independent league called the Continental League. This league had no connection with the one Branch Rickey tried to start in the late fifties. It was formed by a fellow named Walter Dilbeck from Evansville, Indiana.

The games were to be played in the Dominican Republic city of Santo Domingo. Teams there represented cities in Japan, Venezuela and Puerto Rico. Two teams were from the U.S.: New York and Los Angeles. Johnny Mize and I were to be co-managers of the New York team.

Before going to the Dominican Republic, we held spring training at Daytona Beach. Then we rode to the Miami airport with one-way tickets to Santo Domingo, not round-trip. That was a big mistake.

The concept of this league might not have been a bad idea in itself, but the timing was definitely wrong. With all the political unrest going on, it was impossible for the players or anyone else connected with the Continental League to concentrate on the game. Every time we stepped out of the ballpark, we saw signs saying "Damn Yankees Go Home." After a while, some of us felt that obeying those signs might not be such a bad idea. A league official actually faked his own kidnapping so that he could get back to the States.

To say the league wasn't doing too well financially in all this turmoil would be an understatement. Finally, Dilbeck came up with some money and paid off the team. Mize and I bought plane tickets back to the U.S.

I'm certainly proud to be a member of the Baseball Hall of Fame. I just wish that it hadn't taken me so damned long to get there. I realize that everybody can't get into the Hall of Fame, but I think that my credentials are as good or better than those of a lot of guys who were already in by the time I hung up my spikes.

I'm very proud of my record as a ballplayer. That's one thing the sportswriters can never take away from me. My place in the record book speaks for itself. I had a lifetime batting average of .300. I went to bat 7,946 times, scored 1,247 runs, drove in 1,304 runs, played in 2,380 games, had 2,383 hits, 413 doubles, 148 triples, 169 home runs and a slugging percentage of .453. I drew 1,019 bases on balls and only struck out 538 times. As an outfielder, my fielding average was .980, and I threw out 152 baserunners in the major leagues. I don't have to look these numbers up, either.

I don't think a lot of the writers, who needed to look my record up, bothered to check it. If they had, I don't think I would have had to endure the hell I went through when those Baseball Writers Association of America members repeatedly failed to vote me in.

For 15 years, I waited, and for 15 years, I was disappointed. I understand that I am the only player who was voted on and turned down for 15 years. I had better than 100 votes all 15 years my name was on the writers' Hall of Fame ballot. Several times I got over 200 votes, but they never voted me in.

My name first appeared on a Hall of Fame ballot in 1967. Five seasons had passed since I'd served as player-manager for the Raleigh Caps. 1981 was the last year the writers voted on me. After those last votes were counted, I still had a four year wait ahead of me. During those years from 1967 until 1985, I had literally thousands and thousands of autograph seekers say to me, "You deserve to be in the Hall of Fame. Why aren't you?"

I would always reply, "You'll have to ask the sportswriters. I have nothing to do with it."

During those years I saw many articles in newspapers insinuating that I was grumpy to writers. Hell, I was never unkind to writers. I never stopped any sportswriter from asking a question. I always gave them my honest opinion. I still do today. The way I feel in my heart is the way I express myself. I didn't always tell people what they wanted to hear, but I didn't pull any punches. I would say that if the damned shoe fits your foot, you've got to wear it. Some of the guys in the press must have taken that the wrong way.

Then I saw a column written by New York sportswriter Dick
Young which said the reason I wasn't in the Hall of Fame was that
I played in an era when there were superstars like Yogi Berra. Now
wait a minute! I liked playing alongside Yogi, and I respect him,
but I don't think it's fair for anybody to say that I was overshad-
owed by him. Just look at my credentials, and then look at his.
Yogi may have hit more home runs than I did, but his .285 batting
average was 15 points below mine. I had more hits, more doubles
and more triples.

For that matter, I'm not ashamed to compare my stat sheets to
those of a lot of superstars of my day. That includes guys who
went into the Hall of Fame with flying colors on an early ballot.
It seems to me that some people figure that if a guy hit home runs,
he deserves to be in the Hall of Fame. But they don't take the
all-around player into consideration. I like the man who can hit,
run, field and throw. If you don't believe me, you can look for
yourself. There are a lot of fellows in Cooperstown with a lot of
home runs, but with lifetime batting averages that were unspec-
tacular if not downright modest.

Don't get me wrong. I'm not jealous of every slugger in there.
I definitely feel that Billy Williams, who played for me at Houston, went on to a Hall of Fame career in the big leagues. He hit
426 home runs, with 2,711 hits and a lifetime average of .290.
With his credentials, I feel that he should have been voted in
sooner. Another man I feel the writers really sold short was Johnny
Mize. Here is a guy with a .312 lifetime average and more home
runs than any other lefthanded hitter in National League history,
and the writers never voted him in. The best curveball hitter I've
ever seen had to wait until the second time his name came up
before the Veterans Committee.

That's exactly the same thing that happened to me. After the
writers turned me down for the last time in 1981, I was ineligible
to be considered by the veterans for three years. When my name
first came up for consideration to that committee in 1984, one
columnist predicted that I'd be in the Hall of Fame by sundown.
It didn't happen that way. They selected Pee Wee Reese and Rick
Farrell instead. After that, the same guy wrote that I'd probably

be overlooked again the next year in favor of Ernie Lombardi and Arky Vaughan.

That's when I decided to write the columnist a letter. In it I asked, "How can you feel that Ernie Lombardi and Arky Vaughan should be chosen for the Hall of Fame over me? I had more runs, more base hits, more doubles, more triples and more home runs than they did. Not only could I hit, but I could run, field and throw. Lombardi could only hit; he couldn't run worth a lick."

Dizzy Dean was one of my greatest supporters as far as my getting into the Hall of Fame. After the writers kept turning me down year after year, he finally said that he wouldn't go back to Cooperstown until they put me in.

He never lived to see the day. The last time I saw him was in the summer of 1974. We were together in Hollywood, where he narrated an account of the 1946 World Series for a television show. We had a nice visit out there. I remember riding with him to the Los Angeles airport, where he caught a plane to Nevada. Old Diz never made it home again. He died of a heart attack in Reno.

My family and my children were also big supporters during this period, and, as I've crept into the "senior citizen" category, they have become even more important to me. All my kids have done well, and I'm terribly proud of them. My daughter Gaye attended North Carolina Wesleyan College and Mississippi State, then got her master's degree from the University of Tennessee. She is married to Randy Remmer, who operates Remmer Electric here in Roxboro. Gaye is an English teacher at Northern Junior High School.

My daughter Sharon graduated from Duke University, lived in New York City for a while, but now is living and working in Raleigh. My youngest daughter Rhonda attended Louisburg College, and went on to graduate from the University of North Carolina at Wilmington. My daughter Patricia lived in Springfield, Illinois, for a number of years but recently has moved to St. Louis, where she works as a promotional director for a cosmetic company. My son Rex is a successful architect in Colorado Springs.

Finally, in March 1985, the Veterans Committee selected me for the Hall of Fame. I had been disappointed for many years, and when I heard the news, I was sure thankful that they saw fit to put me in. I understand that Bob Broeg, who is on that committee, really went to bat for me. Stan Musial was also on that committee and, of course, I played against a majority of the men in that group. They knew what I could do in a ballgame.

Along with me, the veterans selected Arky Vaughan posthumously. I had told folks that if I had to go in posthumously, I wasn't going in at all. Of course Arky was only 40 years old when he drowned, so at least he didn't have to go through the disappointment year after year of being turned down. Anyway, I was finally in, and in good company. Earlier that year, the writers voted in Lou Brock and Hoyt Wilhelm.

As soon as it became official that I had been selected by the Veterans Committee, I was flown to St. Petersburg, where I appeared at a press conference. I said that I felt a lot of sportswriters from New York did me an injustice by writing a lot of things about me that weren't true. I resented the fact that I had been accused of spiking Jackie Robinson. I didn't like being called an instigator of a strike, especially one that never happened. I feel it was these lies that had kept me out of the Hall of Fame for so long.

Like everyone else, I have an opinion on the Pete Rose issue. Pete Rose has more hits than anyone else who played the game of baseball. No one can say that he's not qualified to be in the Hall of Fame. You can't keep him out as far as his credentials are concerned. But now, it looks like they're not going to let him in on account that he is said to have gambled on his baseball team.

That's another reason why I say that the Hall of Fame selection is a damned popularity contest. If people look at the merits of a man's record and then go from there, I think you'll see a better representation at Cooperstown. A man's personal life should have nothing to do with his going into the Hall of Fame.

I was married five times and some of the writers may have held that against me. But, hey, that isn't anybody's damned business but Enos Slaughter's.

I was also glad to see Gaylord Perry finally get in. He won over three hundred games, but he had been voted down a few times. Some of the writers hinted that he was being held out because he used foreign substances on the ball to make it slippery. But, if you ask me, he played the game fair and square. What the heck. Let them bring back the spitter. They've taken so much out of baseball now that it's getting to be downright pitiful. A pitcher can't knock a guy down anymore. A runner can't slide out of the baseline to break up a double play. It's really getting to be a puny game.

Today, if a guy rips two or three home runs and the next pitch comes close to him, he falls out of the batter's box and cries. Guys like that should have played back in the '30s and '40s. He'd have been knocked down every time he came up to the plate. And he wouldn't have opened his mouth about it or he would have been knocked down again.

Of course, I still follow baseball. I'd have to say that the only players that I really like to see play are George Brett and Don Mattingly. Every time they take the field, they go out there to play hard-nosed baseball. They don't go out there to put on. There's no showboating or acting from them. They just swing the bat and run and play the game like it should be played.

The game has changed a lot, of course. None of the players had agents back in my day. Stan Musial had a business manager when he was still playing, but that was after I had been traded from the Cardinals.

I don't know if I'd want to use an agent. Look at these agents today. They get their percentage of the player's salary before he gets any. Some of the big-salaried modern players file for bankruptcy right after their playing career is over. They may have made over a million dollars a year, but as soon as they can't play anymore, they're broke. There's something wrong there somewhere. The agents must not be handling their money right. It's a shame to see bad investments wipe out all the money a player has earned on the field.

I was inducted into the Hall of Fame on July 25, 1985. I've returned to Cooperstown for the induction ceremony every year since. I hope to keep going back as long as I live.

To me, there's no excuse for a Hall-of-Famer not to attend the ceremony each summer. Some of them don't, but I can't understand why, unless they are in bad health. Usually that is not the case. I realize that a lot of these guys work. Many are still in baseball. But, hell, there's not a team in the major leagues that wouldn't let them off to come to the Hall of Fame. I've noticed that some of the fellows take time off to play in Equitable Old Timers Games in the different cities, but they can't take off to go to Cooperstown, the town where they received the highest honor you can get in baseball.

Of course, ballplayers get paid to participate in an Equitable Old Timers Game; they don't get any fee to come to Cooperstown. But those folks still take care of you. The Hall of Fame pays the flight expenses for two people. In past trips, I have taken two of my daughters and my brother Robert. In addition to round-trip plane tickets and a room at the Otesaga Hotel, we are picked up at the Syracuse Airport and chauffered to Cooperstown.

I hope to see the day when I will be there with all the living members. I definitely feel that there's a way we could all come back and help honor the new members. As long as my health will let me, I'll always go back to Cooperstown and gladly be counted among that number. Charlie Gehringer is 87 years old, and I don't think he's missed one induction ceremony since 1949, when they let him in.

I don't think Enos Slaughter is ever going to miss one, either.